People

Yearbook

2012

Contents . 2011

4

14

78

38

92

46

Music

Fashion

Farewell

104

News&Events

No affair got more press, and drew more weepy watchers, than the unforgettable royal wedding

William
&
Catherine

April 29, 2011 ■ *LONDON*

Will and Kate Say "I do"

It was the royal weddingpalooza all of England—and haberdashers everywhere—had been waiting for, as the future King and Queen finally wed

IN A SMALL, SIMPLE CEREMONY ATTENDED BY A few close friends and family, Prince Will and Kate Middleton tied the knot on … no wait, that's not quite right. Let's try again: In a 766-year-old church where Kipling and Dickens are buried, before 1,900 dignitaries and dozens of heads of state, with more than a million people swarming the streets of London for a peek and tens of millions around the world watching on TV, a couple of crazy-in-love kids got hitched. The April 29 nuptials of Prince William and Kate Middleton in Westminster Abbey—the most anticipated and spectacular wedding since Will's mom, Diana, wed Prince Charles 30 years earlier—were the Oscars of Anglophilia, the Super Bowl of

satin and lace and the World Cup of wacky hats all rolled into one.

Together for eight years before Will finally proposed during a Kenyan holiday in 2010, the couple somehow managed a wedding that delivered all the necessary pomp and pageantry but also had, said one guest, "an incredibly friendly feel to it." Kate, 29, kept the identity of her dress designer a secret until the last possible moment, adding to the drama when she finally emerged from London's Goring hotel in a stunning lace and ivory gown by Sarah Burton for Alexander McQueen (and a Cartier halo tiara). Will, 28, wore the traditional scarlet uniform of the Colonel of the Irish Guards and seemed genuinely dazzled as his bride-to-

WHERE'S WALDO? More than a million people packed London , with thousands lining the route that brought Will and Kate in an open carriage from Westminster Abbey to Buckingham Palace, and huge crowds huddled outside the palace to witness the couple's first kiss.

I, WILLIAM ARTHUR PHILIP LOUIS, TAKE THEE, CATHERINE ELIZABETH, TO MY WEDDED WIFE, TO HAVE AND TO HOLD FROM THIS DAY FORWARD"

PIP, PIP, HOORAY!
Pippa Middleton carried her sister's train into Westminster Abbey—and nearly eclipsed Kate with her own showy dress.

THE HANDOFF
Kate's father, Michael, delivered a beaming Kate to her betrothed at Westminster Abbey.

❝

THEY'RE DEFINITELY
A TEAM. THEY ASK EACH
OTHER, 'SHOULD WE DO
SO-AND-SO?' YOU CAN
JUST SEE IT" —A GUEST

▪SHE WAS AMUSED
A cheerful Queen Elizabeth, in
a bright primrose dress, and Prince
Philip arrive at Buckinghamd Palace
ahead of the bride and groom.

▪IS HE NEXT?
A dashing Prince Harry
called Will "the perfect
brother" during his
reception speech,
according to an insider.

▪PROUD PAPA
Will's father, Prince Charles,
(with wife Camilla) gave
a toast in honor of his new
"lovely daughter" Kate

be swept down the Abbey's endless aisle. When the Archbishop of Canterbury declared them man and wife, the joyful roar of tens of thousands watching on TV screens outside reverberated through the stone walls of the church. "There was a swell of smiles and laughter when the cheers came from outside," says one of the guests, Kate Wright. "The congregation almost wanted to join in the cheering."

Yet the vows were a mere prelude to the day's most heart-stopping moment: when Will and Kate appeared on the balcony of Buckingham Palace and—with throngs watching and waiting—kissed not once but *twice*, a perhaps unprecedented public display of affection in the annals of royal family history. Later,

they took a surprise spin through London in a 1969 Aston Martin convertible festooned with balloons and the license plate "JU5T WED." The day had its shining turns by supporting players—a playful Prince Harry keeping his brother loose at the altar (before accepting the mantle of the UK's most eligible bachelor) and Kate's lovely sister Pippa emerging as a fashion star in her own form-hugging Sarah Burton creation.

The newlyweds danced to the Beatles' "She Loves You" at a rousing reception capped by fireworks— a brilliant end to a truly breathtaking day. Together Will and Kate will be "the King and Queen of the people," said Diana's friend and wedding guest Lana Marks. "This is going to be a great love story."

■**THE HAPPY COUPLE**
Will and Kate wave to the huge crowds outside Buckingham Palace. "They are not stuffy people," says Will's former press secretary Colleen Harris. "They are unpompous and open."

■**WILL & KATE'S WILD RIDE**
The couple's open-air spin in an Aston Martin "showed their sense of fun," said one guest. "They're a cool young couple."

The undersea earthquake that triggered disaster shifted the tilt of Earth, increased the speed of its spin and even shortened the length of the day by fractions of a second. The tsunami that struck the coast of Japan one hour later on March 11 with tidal waves up to three stories high, its flood waters reaching as far as six miles inland, caused devastation of Biblical proportions, flattening towns, carrying away bridges and trains and causing meltdowns at three nuclear reactors. The World Bank estimated losses could reach $235 billion, making it the costliest natural disaster in history. But the human toll—more than 15,700 dead and 4,000 missing—was expressed in the tears of survivors like 21-year-old Yui Sawaguchi, who tried desperately to reach her mother in coastal Sendai, only to find "the whole town was swept away and vanished."

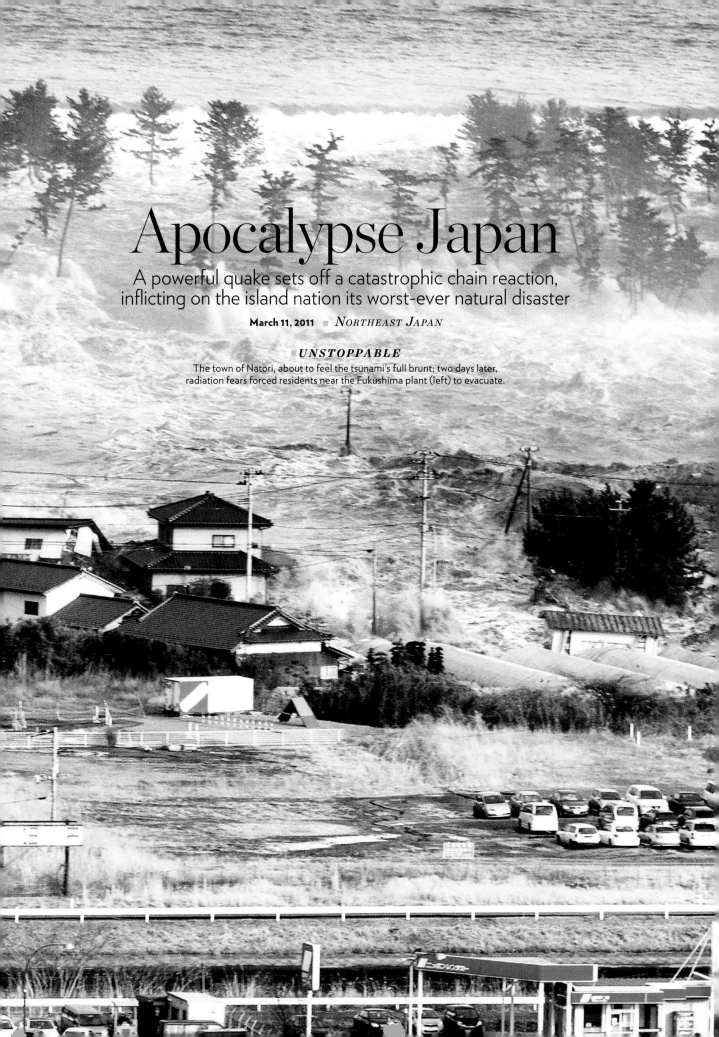

Apocalypse Japan

A powerful quake sets off a catastrophic chain reaction,
inflicting on the island nation its worst-ever natural disaster

March 11, 2011 ■ *Northeast Japan*

■ *UNSTOPPABLE*

The town of Natori, about to feel the tsunami's full brunt; two days later,
radiation fears forced residents near the Fukushima plant (left) to evacuate.

Casey Anthony: Shocking Verdict

June and July 2011 ▪ *ORLANDO*

Not since O.J. Simpson has an accused killer so transfixed the media— and a verdict so startled the nation

SHE STOOD ACCUSED OF UNSPEAKABLE EVIL— murdering her 2-year-old daughter Caylee simply to make her own life easier. She had to answer for unthinkable actions—not reporting her daughter's disappearance for a month, partying in nightclubs in the weeks after Caylee went missing. And so, on judgment day, Casey Anthony nervously bit her nails as she waited for 12 jurors to deliver her fate. Would they conclude—as millions across the country already had—that Anthony was, beneath her elfin, inscrutable exterior, a monster?

The case against Anthony, 25, a Florida single mother, seemed damning. Why, after her parents discovered Caylee was missing in 2008, did Anthony lie to police about a nonexistent nanny? Why, if Caylee accidentally drowned, as Anthony later insisted, was her body found with duct tape sealing her mouth? Why was "chloroform" googled on the Anthony home computer in the days before Caylee vanished? Yet for all of Anthony's bizarre behavior there was no direct evidence linking her to the murder—no blood, no DNA, no witness. Prosecutors, claimed her attorney Jose Baez, were relying on "fantasy forensics." Even her agonized parents, George and Cindy—who admitted in court that Casey lied to them about what happened to Caylee—fell far short of ever admitting they believed their daughter was guilty.

Around midday on July 5, after a six-week televised trial and only 10 hours of deliberation, the jury found Anthony not guilty of killing Caylee. She wept and hugged her attorneys; outside the Orlando courthouse, shocked spectators called for justice. "I wish we had more evidence to put her away," one juror later said. Two weeks after the verdict, Anthony was set free, and she's now in hiding in Florida and seeking psychiatric treatment, according to her lawyers. "She hopes she will someday redeem herself," says someone close to her, "and live a productive life." The dark secrets at the heart of her case may forever remain just that—secrets. "We don't know any more today about what happened to Caylee than we did the day they found her body," says noted Orlando defense attorney Richard Hornsby. "And we may never know."

◼ *VICTIM OR KILLER?*

Casey Anthony with her lawyers Jose Baez and Dorothy Clay Sims in the moments before she was found not guilty of first-degree murder, child abuse and manslaughter (above). From far left: Judge Belvin Perry; a spectator reacts to Anthony's acquittal; Casey's parents, George and Cindy Anthony, at a memorial ceremony for Caylee; mourners left cards, flowers and stuffed animals in the Orlando woods where young Caylee's body was found.

▪ PASSION!
Before they met on
Cleopatra, Taylor vowed
to be "the one leading
lady that Richard Burton
will never get." Wrong!

SPECTACLE!
Everything about *Cleopatra* was epic,
including the Roman Forum set,
bigger than the real thing; Taylor's
$1 million salary, the highest in
Hollywood; and the film's legendary
box-office belly flop.

Elizabeth Taylor

1932-2011 ▪ *Los Angeles, Calif.*

Passion, scandals, weddings,
chalets, casts of thousands
and diamonds as big
as the Ritz: *That* was a star

I have lived every second,"
Elizabeth Taylor once
said—and she had the
stories, scars and jewelry to
prove it. The movie goddess
was married eight times,
accused of "erotic vagrancy"
by the Vatican, given gems
worth tens of millions of
dollars, befriended by kings and
tycoons, and became addicted
to alcohol and painkillers—
a breathless soap opera she
never seemed to tire of starring
in. "I've been lucky all my life,"
said the actress, who died at 79
of complications from congestive
heart failure. "Everything was
handed to me: looks, fame,
wealth, honors, love. But I've
paid for that luck with disasters.
Terrible illnesses, destructive
addictions, broken marriages."
Said her friend Larry King:
"We lost the last of what can
truly be called a star."

■ THE TAYLOR EFFECT

"She was the most beautiful child I ever saw," said pal Roddy McDowell. Taylor (above, ca. 1955) could have an even more powerful effect as an adult: Frequent husband Richard Burton described her as "an erotic legend...whose breasts could topple empires."

Happy Trails

Exiting after 25 years, Oprah gives fans a star-powered group hug

FOR TWO DAYS RUNNING, *The Oprah Winfrey Show* featured a blinding celebrity lineup. Aretha, Madonna and Beyoncé sang her praises; Tom Hanks and Halle Berry bowed before her; Hoops King Michael Jordan and, yes, Couch King Tom Cruise joined the love fest. But it was her final guest who outshone them all on May 25 when, after a quarter century of inspiring words, self-affirming makeovers, big-ticket giveaways and hard-won life lessons—"Don't wait for somebody else to complete you," she said—Oprah stood alone onstage with a tear and a smile. "I won't say goodbye," she said. "I'll just say, 'Until we meet again.'"

Jennifer Aniston
& Justin Theroux

Friends say the costars in love see family in their future

Back in February, Jennifer Aniston looked into her crystal ball and liked what she saw. "There are all sorts of things that are going to be happening in the near future, so I'm excited," she told PEOPLE. As it happened, love, in the person of screenwriter (*Tropic Thunder, Iron Man 2*) and actor (*Parks and Recreation*) Justin Theroux, was right around the corner. The couple, who met the summer before on the set of *Wanderlust*, began dating in May; their romance was in full bloom by June when they appeared for their public unveiling at an MTV Movie Awards party in L.A. "I'm extremely lucky and extremely happy," Aniston said during a visit to New York with her new beau later that month.

Before the summer was out, Theroux had been introduced to those nearest and dearest, including Courteney Cox and dad John Aniston, she had sold her Beverly Hills mansion (letting it go for $38 million, $4 million less than her pre-romance asking price) and the two were cohabiting in a modest love nest in the Hollywood Hills.

THE OTHER WOMAN

Housekeeper Mildred Baena, 50, said she never told Schwarzenegger he was the father of her son Joseph, 14. The truth began to emerge, she told *Hello!* magazine, when she began bringing Joseph, who resembles Arnold, to the family's home in 2010.

Arnold's Secret

A Hollywood political power couple's shocking split

They seemed, every inch, a team, "devoted and in love with each other regardless of whatever external noise there was," said someone who worked closely with former California Governor Arnold Schwarzenegger, 64, and his wife, Maria Shriver, 56. "He leaned on her, she leaned on him, and they laughed a lot." When accusations of sexual shenanigans threatened his candidacy in 2003, Maria was fierce in her husband's defense: "I am my own woman," she told Oprah Winfrey. "I have not been quote 'bred' to look the other way. I look at that man … eyes wide open, and I look at him with an open heart."

All of which made the revelation that, 14 years ago, Schwarzenegger had fathered a child with Mildred Baena, one of the family's housekeepers, even more heartbreaking. "There are no excuses," said Schwarzenegger, "and I take full responsibility for the hurt I have caused…. I am truly sorry." In July, Shriver filed for divorce.

■ **ON HER WATCH**
Murdoch had *News* editor Rebekah Brooks's back, but cops had her arrested.

■ **WITH APOLOGIES**
Murdoch's son James (right), 39 and News Corp.'s deputy chief operating officer, sat at the Boss's side during initial questioning by British lawmakers.

Hacking Scandal Scalds Media Czar

PAST ALLEGATIONS THAT reporters on his beloved Fleet Street scandal sheets had hacked the phones of the Royal Family and celebrities like Jude Law and Gwyneth Paltrow barely caused a ripple in media baron Rupert Murdoch's sprawling empire. But News Corporation, which counts FOX News and *The Wall Street Journal* among its U.S. holdings, was rocked to its foundations when it was alleged that among the targets of his *News of the World* snoops were families of British servicemen killed in Iraq and a 13-year-old murder victim, Milly Dowler, whose voice-mail messages, deleted by reporters, might have proved crucial to the police investigation. The aftershocks included the closing of the *News of the World*, the demise of Mudoch's $12 billion bid to buy the British Sky Broadcasting network and outrage that led to Murdoch's televised grilling by members of Parliament. "This is the most humble day of my life," he said. Perhaps not: Although 16 have been arrested so far, the investigation continues.

Death of a Terrorist

May 1, 2011 ▪ *WASHINGTON, D.C.*

Absolute secrecy,
courageous decision, daring
raid, stunning result

THE RISKS WERE IMMENSE: The lives of 23 U.S. Navy SEALs;
American prestige abroad; and, for President Obama,
arguably, the next election. But the prize, 9/11 mastermind
Osama bin Laden, was worth it. On April 29, Obama made
the courageous call; two days later, the SEALs, in a lightning
raid 120 miles into Pakistan, attacked bin Laden's compound
in Abbotabad, killed the terrorist and four of his supporters,
gathered up invaluable papers and computer hard drives, and
escaped without casualties.

Afterward, Obama addressed the nation. "We will be
relentless in defense of our citizens," he said. "And on nights
like this one, we can say to those families who have lost loved
ones to al-Qaeda's terror: Justice has been done."

For John Travolta and Kelly Preston, whose son Jett, 16, passed away in 2009, the arrival of Benjamin Travolta, 8 lbs. 3 oz., was a joy almost beyond words. "For us, it's been uplifting," said Travolta. "He's given the house a renewed spirit and purpose. He's brought us a new beginning, and his presence has brought joy to all the people who have wanted the best for us." Preston, 48, says that she and Travolta, 56, after trying for three years, had begun to think "maybe it wasn't possible for us." Now, she says, Benjamin's sister Ella Blue, 10, "can't stop kissing him and keeps saying, 'Oh, he's so cute!' "

John Travolta
&
Kelly Preston

BENJAMIN ■ **November 23, 2010**

The couple and their daughter welcome
a small miracle named Benjamin

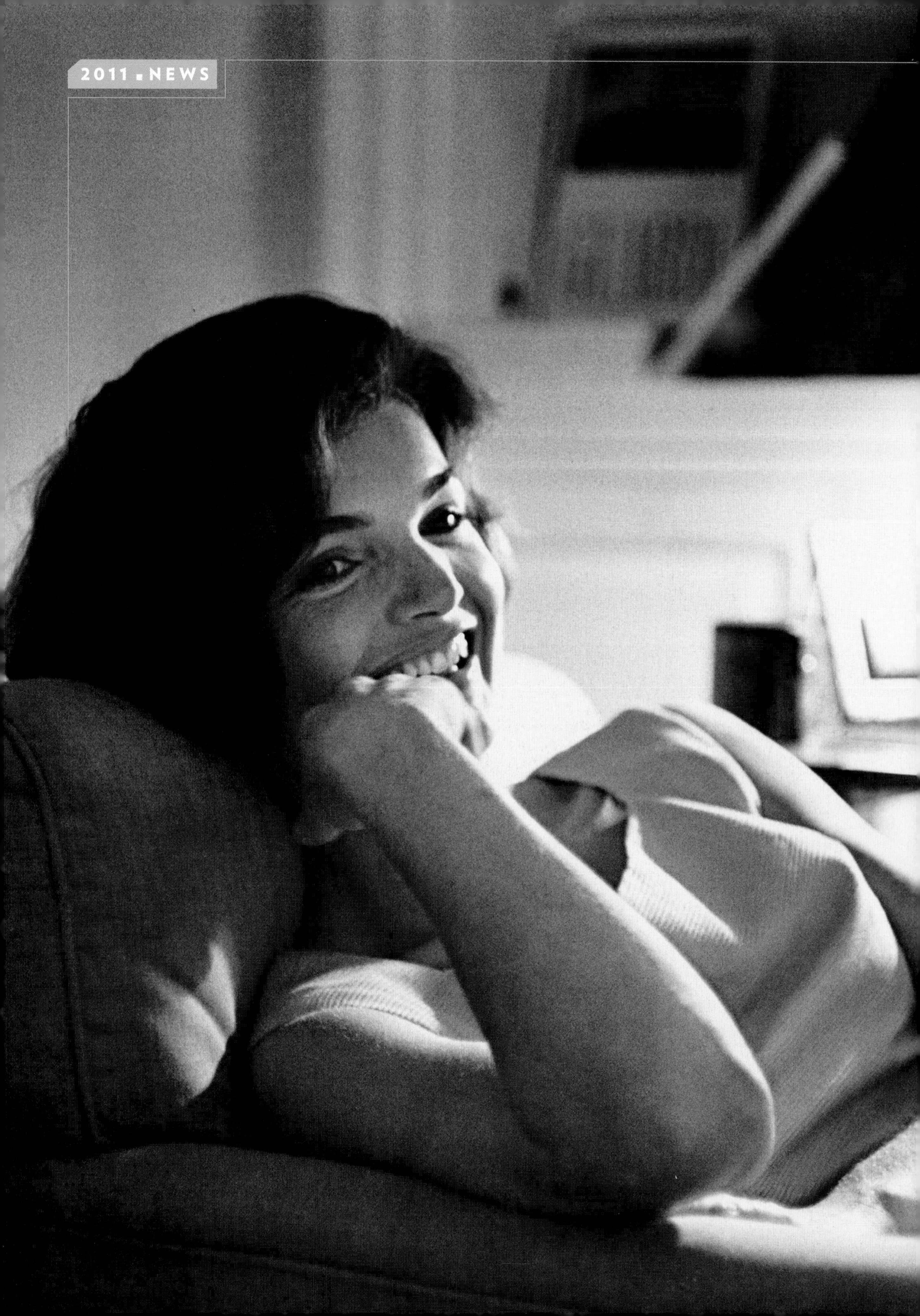

Jackie Speaks

"MOST PEOPLE CAN IDENTIFY my mother instantly," writes Caroline Kennedy, "but they really don't know her at all." They'll know her a lot better after reading *Jacqueline Kennedy: Historic Conversations on Life with John F. Kennedy,* based on extraordinarily revealing interviews the former First Lady gave to historian Arthur Schlesinger Jr. in 1964 that were kept private until now (her daughter wrote the preface). Kennedy shows herself to be smart, opinionated and not at all shy about firing back at people, no matter how powerful, whom she perceived as hypocritical or unkind to her husband (the effect is even more dramatic in the audio version of the book, where her whispering, little-girl voice is often in striking contrast to the force of her words). Some samples:

ON LBJ: JFK told Jackie, "Oh God, can you ever imagine what would happen to the country if Lyndon were President?"

THE FEMALE VOTE: Jackie thought women who preferred JFK's onetime rival Adlai Stevenson were "scared of sex . . . these sort of twisted poor little women whose lives hadn't work out . . . Jack made them nervous."

ON MAMIE EISENHOWER: "You know, there was this sort of venom or something there."

ON MARTIN LUTHER KING: After Jackie heard that he had once arranged for an orgy and had "made fun of Cardinal Cushing" at JFK's funeral, she said, "I just can't see a picture without thinking, you know, that man's terrible."

THE WOMAN BEHIND THE MAN: Jackie saw her role as "making it always a climate of affection and comfort and détente when [Jack] came home . . . good food and the children in good moods." Despite everything, the White House years, she said, were "the happiest time of my life."

Non-Weeping Willow Goes Viral

April 2, 2011 ▪ *Los Angeles*

NOT SINCE RAPUNZEL have tresses been such a boon to their owner. "It's very, very amazing," acknowledged Willow Smith, 10—Will and Jada Pinkett Smith's hyperprecocious daughter—whose hit single put $4 million (!) in her piggy bank, scored her a recording contract and inspired a great spoof by Jimmy Fallon and Bruce Springsteen. And if anybody's jealous, Smith could quote the song's lyrics: "Don't let haters keep me off my grind."

Charlie Sheen's Wild Ride

Where, oh where, to start? The claim that he overcame years of drug problems by waking up with "a new brain?" That he's a "warlock," "ninja" and "total rock star from Mars," his enemies are "retarded zombies" and "trolls," and that, even at nearly $2 million a week, he was underpaid for turning the sitcom *Two and a Half Men* from a "tin can" into "gold"? Charlie Sheen's Hunter S. Thompson–esque rants helped get him fired from that show after eight seasons—to which he responded with a lawsuit, and another rant: "At some point there is nothing to say. Only war to wage. Without judgment. Without fear … The winds are howling tonight. The gods are hungry. The beast is alive. And awake. And deadly."

The most mind-boggling turn? On September 26, Sheen and Warner Bros. Television agreed to a reported $25 million settlement, and the Great War simply … stopped.

■ ONE MAN'S 24/7 CRUSADE

Sheen ranted freely via a home-produced video feed (top), eventually cobbled together a rag-tag show dubbed My Violent Torpedo of Truth Tour, and performed (right) in 20 cities, often introducing his "goddesses" (Rachel Oberlin, above left, and Natalie Kenly), the two women with whom he was then living. By September, Sheen seemed to have calmed down, presenting an Emmy and wishing Two and a Half Men "nothing but the best for this upcoming season."

Steve Jobs

He taught the world to think differently about music, movies, work and life

October 5, 2011 ■ *PALO ALTO, CALIF.*

"PUT A DENT IN THE UNIVERSE," he used to say, exhorting his colleagues to excel. The visionary Zen Master of Tech—who brightened the world by bringing to life the Apple computer and the Mac, the iPod, iPhone and iPad and oh, yes, Buzz Lightyear and the digital animation gang from Pixar—came as close as any earthbound geek can to leaving his mark (okay, Mac mouse print) in the cosmos. "In a world littered with dull objects, he brought the beauty of clean lines and clear thought," U2's Bono said of his friend, who died at 56 from pancreatic cancer. Born to grad school students, who put him up for adoption, and raised in a blue-collar Bay Area family, Jobs turned presumed wrong turns—he dropped both LSD and out of college in his early 20s; fathered a child out of wedlock and managed to get himself fired from Apple nine years after he founded it—into a career path of unparalleled success.

A Deadly Day in Afghanistan

August 6, 2011 ▪ *TANGI VALLEY, AFGHANISTAN*

THREE MONTHS AFTER COMRADES carried out the attack on Osama bin Laden, 22 Navy SEALs, along with 8 Army and Air Force troops, 7 Afghan commandos and a civilian interpreter were killed when a Chinook helicopter carrying them on a mission against a Taliban stronghold was shot down by a rocket-propelled grenade. The toll, 38, made it the deadliest event for U.S. forces in the war. "My heart is breaking," said the widow of a SEAL killed in 2010. "I know what is going on in those families."

▪ Brian Bill, 31, loved music "from Beethoven to Metallica."

▪ Patrick Hamburger, 31, a first-time dad.

▪ Kevin Houston, 35, "was born to do this job," says his mom, Jan Brown.

▪ Michael Strange, 25, hoped to be a nurse.

Chris Campbell, 36, a jock who loved to serve.

▪ John Brown, 33, Bronze Star recipient.

Nightmare in Tucson

January 8, 2011 ■ *TUCSON, ARIZ.*

The event was a routine meet-and-greet at a supermarket—until Jared Loughner, 22, walked up to congresswoman Gabrielle Gifford's, shot her in the head, then turned his Glock pistol on the crowd, killing 6, including Christina Green, a 9-year-old girl born on Sept. 11, 2001, and wounding 12 others. The nightmarish attack inspired fierce debate about gun control and the toxicity of current political dialogue. Miraculously surviving her wound, Gifford's, after months of painful therapy, received a standing ovation from both sides of the aisle when she returned to congress on Aug. 1 and cast her vote to raise the nation's debt ceiling.

■ THE CALM KILLER

Top: Tending the wounded after the Oslo bombing; above, Anders Breivik after his arrest. Right: Mourners leave flowers on a shore facing Utøya island. "The worst were the seconds when I heard him reloading," said one victim, shot in both thighs and one shoulder. "What saved me was that he thought I was dead. Seven of the 10 in the room were killed."

Tragedy in Norway

July 22, 2011 ■ *Oslo and Utøya Island, Norway*

FIRST, A BOMB EXPLODED in Oslo, outside the building that houses the Norwegian prime minister's office. Ninety minutes later, a 6-ft.-tall blond man dressed as a policeman arrived on nearby Utøya island, home to a Labor Party camp for teenagers, raised an assault rifle and opened fire. "I watched as he slowly lifted up tent flaps and shot the people inside," recalled one young staffer, who was wounded in the shoulder. "At one point four people approached him, thinking he was a real policeman. I saw one of them say, 'Thank you, you've come to help us.' He shot all four of them." When a SWAT team arrived an hour later, Anders Behring Breivik, 32, a rabidly conservative, anti-immigrant fanatic, calmly surrendered; he later confessed to the bombing as well. He has been charged in the deaths of 77 people—the most violent day in Norway since WWII.

Wannabe pop star Rebecca Black's Freaky "Fridays" moment

REBECCA BLACK, 13, WAS a typical Anaheim, Calif., eighth-grader—until a YouTube video of her singing a song called "Fridays" went viral. Haters—and they were legion—heralded the mindless, Auto-tuned bit of fluff as emblematic of all that was wrong with pop music, if not an early sign of the coming of the Apocalypse. But Black, in the end, had the last laugh: "Fridays" had 167 million views on YouTube.

■ *SHOCKED*
Weiner's wife, Huma Abedin, was pregnant when the scandal broke.

Famous Weiner becomes big loser

SIMPLE RULE: IF YOU are a congressman, *do not e-mail pictures of your private parts to random women.* How could (now former) Rep. Anthony Weiner not know this?

From the firestorm sparked by her best-seller *Battle Hymn of the Tiger Mother,* you'd think Amy Chua had done the unthinkable: deprived her kids of their God-given right to watch TV. In fact, the Chinese-

Mom's a Tiger

A parenting book triggers a debate over the author's tough-love demands for excellence

American mother-of-two *also* banned sleepovers, video games, sports and school plays. After-school hours in the Tiger Mom's den were devoted to homework and music lessons (older daughter Sophia gave a violin recital at Carnegie Hall at 14).

Chua's charges had to practice just to get a bathroom break. "Parents like Amy Chua are the reason why Asian-Americans like me are now in therapy," blogged one critic. "The immigrant approach," Chua maintains, "is about making kids the best they can be."

▪ SMILING WITH MILEY
Billy Ray, Miley and Tish Cyrus in L.A. in March 2010. He and Miley bonded over "this freak show" of fame, Billy Ray said, "but everything has a price."

Cyrus Family: Achey-Breaky Hearts

LOOKING BACK, it was a slow-building storm: Disney star Miley Cyrus, then 15, photographed, draped in a satin stole, for *Vanity Fair*. Shots of her, scantily clad, pop up on the web. Ditto a video of her giving a lap dance to a film producer. When a photo surfaced of her smoking a bong (filled, she said, with the legal psychoactive herb salvia), her dad, singer Billy Ray Cyrus, tweeted forlornly,

"Sorry, guys. I had no idea. There is much beyond my control right now." Weeks later he dropped a bombshell: Claiming fame had "destroyed my family," he filed for divorce from Tish, his wife of 17 years. Days later the storm subsided. "It is very important for me to work on mending my family right now," Billy Ray told PEOPLE. In March he called off the divorce.

▪ UPBEAT
Mason, with 17 pins in his legs, took four months to recover but always stayed "happy and sweet" said a caretaker.

Mason the Wonderdog

SUCKED OUT OF A GARAGE by the April 27 tornadoes that ravaged Alabama, Mason, a terrier mix, was presumed lost—until, three weeks later, on two severely broken legs, he crawled back to his owner's porch, wagging his tail. Only Mason knows "how far he crawled," said a rescue worker, "and he's not talking."

Sandra gets her groove back

Few have ever had to cope with that magnitude of emotional whiplash: One moment Sandra Bullock was winning a Golden Globe (and thanking her husband, saying, "I never knew what it felt like for someone to have my back") and an Oscar; eight days later, reports surfaced that her man, biker Jesse James, had been two-timing her with a tattooed stripper. Devastated, she filed for divorce and hunkered down. But that was 2010. The new year saw her regain her footing in style. "Her No. 1 priority is her son, Louis Bardo," said a source. "No. 2 is work." She filmed two movies, *Extremely Loud and Incredibly Close,* and *Gravity* with George Clooney. As for romance, gossips matched her with longtime pal Ryan Reynolds, but Bullock, denied the link with impish élan: "He is not my *lovah,*" she said. "I don't get his loving after dark."

■ *BACK ON THE CARPET*
Bullock showed for the August premier of Ryan Reynolds' *The Change-Up*, but friends said the pair, who costarred in 2009's *The Proposal,* are just pals. They'll reteam for an action comedy, *Most Wanted.*

Meg's Surprise

THE YEAR'S MOST out-of-left-field celeb romance? Perhaps former romcom queen Meg Ryan, 50, and rocker John Mellencamp, 60. Ryan, who has shunned the spotlight for a decade, has been spotted with the recently divorced Mellencamp (his 18-year marriage to model Elaine Irwin ended in August) on Martha's Vineyard and New York. The attraction? Meg is "not the cutie-pie she appeared onscreen," says a Hollywood source. "She really liked...rough-and-ready guys' guys."

My Bad, Says Brad

Talking to *Parade,* Brad Pitt said that for years he felt stuck in a rut, and "my marriage [to Jennifer Aniston] had something to do with it." The comment left him backpedaling like Lance Armstrong attacking an alp in reverse: "Jen is an incredibly giving, loving and hilarious woman who remains my friend," he said, by way of clarification. "The point I was trying to make is not that Jen was dull, but that I was becoming dull to myself … and that, I am responsible for."

Baby, you can drive my truck? On Oct. 9, Sir Paul McCartney, 69, married Nancy Shevell, 51, an executive at her father's New Jersey-based trucking company, at the Old Marylebone Town Hall in London. The low-key and private Shevell ("I'm over 50, I work, that's it—there really isn't much to talk about") and the Cute One met a few summers ago in East Hampton, N.Y., where McCartney has a home. "He doesn't like a big social life, nor does she," notes her cousin, journalist Barbara Walters. Says Rita Wilson, who, with husband Tom Hanks, is a friend of the newlyweds: "They're both so real. That's why they're so good for each other. It's a very happy story." One good sign? Paul's designer daughter Stella—who, along with her sisters, reportedly did not get on well with his ex, Heather Mills—created Shevell's wedding dress.

He Loves Her,
Yeah Yeah Yeah

He won Best Urban/Alternative Performance at this year's Grammys for his hit "Forget You"; next year, if they give a Special Effects Grammy, Cee Lo Green should be a shoe-in. At the Billboard Awards in May, the innovative entertainer performed a medley of songs while his mirrored piano levitated, hovered and, as he continued singing, did a complete 360 in the air. Now *that's* entertainment.

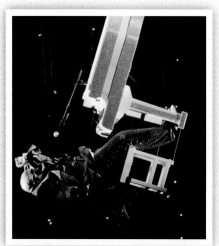

Star Tracks

Spinning pianos, an extra-large Elvis and a red-carpet monkey: memorable photos of 2010

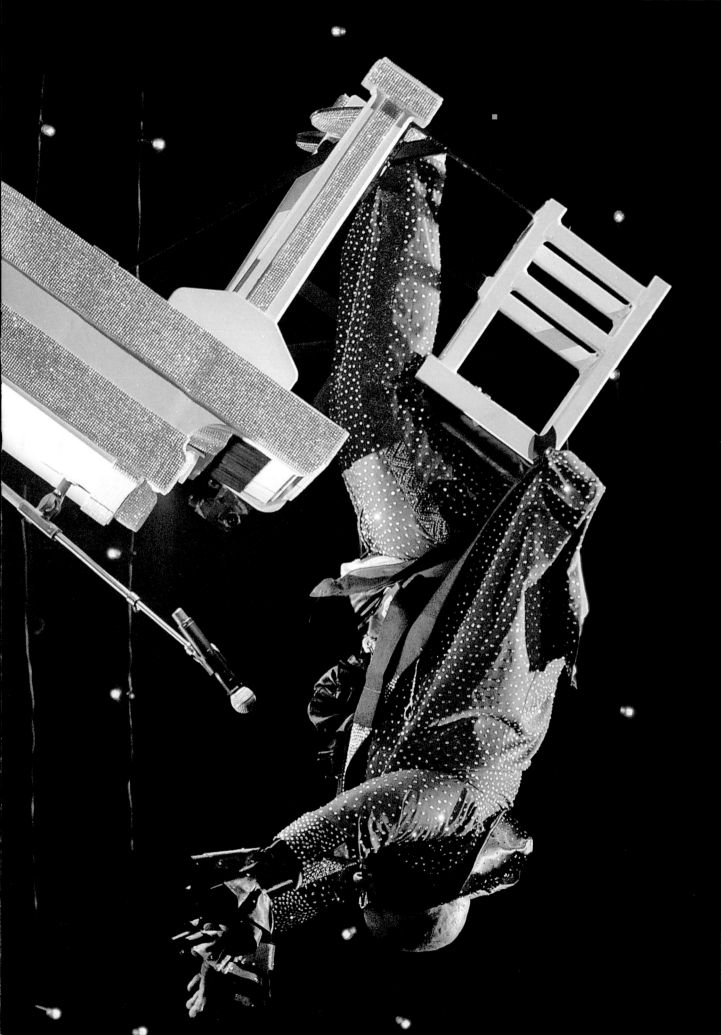

■ *AVAST, ETC.*
Johnny Depp and his movie
dad, Keith Richards, smiled
for the cameras at the
premiere of *Pirates of the
Caribbean: On Stranger Tides*.
Is there more of this sort of
thing in the Rolling Stone's
future? Joked Richards: "You
should see my King Lear."

■ **THE NOT-SO-INVISIBLE MAN**
It looked like Dustin Hoffman, ostrich-like, picked the wrong tree to hide behind while dodging paparazzi in L.A. Actually, he was just kidding around with the lensmen.

■ **ON THE ROOF**
No longer on TV, former *John and Kate Plus Eight* star John Gosselin returned to the job as a construction worker.

Gaga Goes Joe

Lady Gaga didn't show at the MTV Video Music Awards, but her alter ego, a guy named Joe Calderone, did. Joe picked up Gaga's awards (Best Female Video and Best Video with a Message), never explained him/herself and never broke character, even at a postshow press conference. Gaga/Calderone described himself as "just a guy" from New Jersey, whose "family's from Palermo, Sicily," and explained, sort of, why he was there instead of her: "She said … 'If you really love me, you'll go instead of me and you'll get in the spotlight.' So I did."

Solid as a Rocker

Tom Cruise, 49, got bulked up, chiseled and ripped to play Stacee Jaxx for the upcoming movie version of the Broadway hit *Rock of Ages*. Noted director Adam Shankman, perhaps hoping to drum up business: "He has zero body fat and is basically naked through the entire movie."

AIR KISS!
Crystal the capuchin, simian star of *The Hangover Part II*, sashayed like a pro at the film's L.A. premiere.

◾ *A HUNKA HUNKA... HUNKA*

It's Vegas, baby: Go big or go home. *Modern Family*'s Eric Stonestreet, channeling the King, opted for the former at the Billboard Music Awards in May.

The Spector of Al Pacino

NEVER ONE TO TURN DOWN A CHALLENGE, Al Pacino (above) is playing murderous record producer Phil Spector—a man with hair even taller than his own—in a movie for HBO written by David Mamet. Further guilding the credits: The role of Spector's defense attorney will be played by Helen Mirren.

Boo, the dog with the do

▪**J.H. LEE'S** friends loved her pooch's look after a groomer stylishly shaved his matted fur, so she posted pix on Facebook. Now Boo has 2 million fans and his own photo book—and no star ego. Says Lee: "He's laid-back and pretty clueless."

BOO
THE LIFE OF THE
WORLD'S CUTEST DOG
by J. H. Lee

Mush, You Huskies!

FRESH FROM LOSING 100 LBS, KIRSTIE ALLEY DID what any newly slim *signora* might do: Flew to Italy and had a team of sculpted studs do her bidding (if only, alas, for a photo shoot). Now that she "has her game again," though, Alley admits that she has men on her mind: "What I'm looking for," she says, "is to be madly, deeply in love."

Hat-tastic!

AFTER THE BALCONY kisses and Pippa's figure, Princess Beatrice's hat was one of the most talked about moments of the royal wedding. She used its powers for good: Its sale, on eBay, raised $130,000 for charity.

Diaz: Not tireless

NOW *THAT'S* ROMANCE: In February, actress Cameron Diaz, 38, and her then-beau, New York Yankee Alex Rodriguez, spent a fun date wrestling enormous tires (presumably, part of A-Rod's regular workout). Check out those biceps!!!

Amanda Knox: Stunning Reversal

IN 2009, AMANDA KNOX, an American studying in Perugia, Italy, was convicted, along with her Italian boyfriend, Raffaele Sollecito, of murdering Knox's roommate, Meredith Kercher, 21, during an evening of sex play gone violently wrong. Portrayed as a "she-devil" and sociopathic sexual adventurer by the Italian press, Knox, then 22, was found guilty largely due to DNA evidence and evasive answers she initially gave police—among other things, she said she had been in the apartment when bar owner Patrick Lumumba had sex with and killed Kercher, even though he was later shown to have an alibi—and was sentenced to 26 years.

In October, with her case on appeal, she stood before a packed courtroom and, before a jury of two judges and six lay people, made a passionate plea in fluent Italian: "I am not what they say … I didn't kill. I didn't rape. I didn't steal," she said. "I am innocent."

To the shock of many, and the delight of family and supporters who had fiercely proclaimed Knox's innocence from day one, the jury—apparently swayed by a report from independent experts that found the DNA evidence to be flawed—agreed, overturning Knox and Sollecito's murder conviction and setting the pair free. Wasting no time, Knox boarded a plane and flew home to Seattle the next day.

■ *FREE, AND NOT*
Sollecito (left) also saw his murder conviction overturned. Rudy Hermann Guede (right), an acquaintance of Kercher's, was tried separately for her murder in 2008, found guilty, and sentenced to 30 years. His sentence was reduced to 16 years in 2009.

■ **WHO KILLED MEREDITH?**
Meredith Kercher's brother Lyle said his family accepted the decision but wondered how a ruling that "was so certain two years ago has been so emphatically overturned." The family's search for justice, he said, "is back at square one."

Crime

Amanda Knox and the West Memphis Three go free; Boston mobster Whitey Bulger gets nabbed; Rod Blagojevich gets convicted

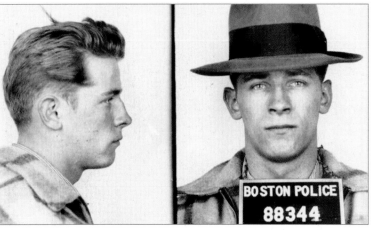

James "Whitey" Bulger
Long Lost, Now Found

AFTER ELUDING A GLOBAL MANHUNT for 15 years, the brutal Boston mob boss wanted for 19 murders fell for a simple ruse. Living anonymously in the Princess Eugenia apartments in Santa Monica, Calif., Bulger, 81, tricked into believing he was the victim of a storage-unit burglary, was arrested on June 22. Neighbors were shocked to learn that the elderly and unsociable putterer had 30 guns and $800,000 in cash stashed in his $1,145 per month apartment. "They seemed poor," one said of Bulger, now jailed in Boston, and his girlfriend. "I felt bad for them."

Call it the he-said/she-said heard 'round the world. On May 14, Dominique Strauss-Kahn, chairman of the International Monetary Fund and, many thought, the next President of France, was arrested and charged with raping Nafissatou Diallo, 32, a housekeeper at Manhattan's Sofitel hotel, where he had been staying in a $3,000-a-night suite. Strauss-Kahn admitted they'd had sex, but insisted it had been consensual; nonetheless, the ugly publicity damaged his effectiveness at the Fund, and he resigned his position. Three months later, prosecutors made a stunning reversal: They dropped all charges—saying that Diallo had lied to them repeatedly about her past and the events surrounding the alleged rape, thus rendering her almost useless as a witness. Strauss-Khan, his reputation shattered—charges of sexual assault of a young Frenchwoman were dropped when the statute of limitation expired—returned to France, where he told an interviewer his interaction with Diallo was "a moral failing…I'm not proud of it."

A Rush to Judgement or Justice Not Done'

Dominique Strauss-Kahn finally flies home

■ 'THE GREAT SEDUCER'

While Nafissatou Diallo (top) accused Strauss-Kahn of rape, his wife, American-born French broadcast journalist Anne Sinclair (with her husband), stood by her man—and also wired $1 million for his bail, flew to New York to be at his side and vehemently protested his innocence. "I do not believe for one second in the accusations brought against my husband," said Sinclair, who surprised even the French when she said that she was "rather proud" of her husband's reputation as a *chaud lapin* ("hot rabbit," or ladies' man). "It's important for a man in politics to be able to seduce," she said.

Sentenced

Guilty verdicts for two politicos

■ ROD BLAGOJEVICH
Headline writers and talk show hosts wept when the Illinois governor known for his bangs, bluster, *Celebrity Apprentice* appearance and boggling belief that voters loved him dearly was convicted June 27 of trying to sell President Obama's former Senate seat and other acts of corruption. One man was surprised: "I frankly am stunned," said Blago.

■ TOM DELAY
When the disgraced Texas congressman known as the Hammer for his hardball tactics stood for sentencing, it was the judge's gavel that packed the real wallop. Convicted in a money laundering scheme, the former House Majority Leader was sentenced to three years in the big house. In August he filed an appeal.

Elizabeth Smart

"I have a wonderful life now," she says as her tormentor is sentenced to spend his in prison

I have forgiven him," she said of Brian David Mitchell, 58 (right), the self-annointed preacher who in 2002 kidnapped and raped her at 14 and held her captive for nine nightmarish months. Now 24, Smart spoke at Mitchell's May sentencing hearing. "But that doesn't mean I have to invite him [to visit] or send little support letters."

The West Memphis Three

Following a long and much-publicized campaign on their behalf, three men, convicted nearly 18 years ago of horrific child murders, are set free

■ **JESSIE MISSKELLEY, 36**
"I told my sister, 'Go, go, go,'" after his Aug. 19 release. "Let's get as far away from here as we can."

■ **JASON BALDWIN, 34**
"We're innocent," he says. "It's obvious to anyone who looks at the facts of the case." He hopes to become a lawyer.

■ **DAMIEN ECHOLS, 36**
He says he was able to endure brutal prison conditions thanks to New Yorker Lorri Davis, a supporter who wed him in 1998.

A MORE UNSPEAKABLE CRIME is hard to imagine: three 8-year-old boys beaten, raped and disfigured with knives, their bodies dumped in a ditch in West Memphis, Ark., in May 1993. With little to implicate them other than they lived nearby, three teens were arrested, tried and convicted after Jessie Misskelley, then 17 and with an IQ of 72, confessed and implicated the others following a 12-hour police interrogation. Supporters, including celebs Natalie Maines, Eddie Vedder and director Peter Jackson, lobbied for years for the trio's freedom; in August the three were released after agreeing to an Alford plea, a complicated legal maneuver that allows them to proclaim their innocence while admitting that there is evidence of guilt.

■ *ON THE LOVE TWAIN*
Embracing her second chance at love,
the country superstar weds Frédéric Thiébaud
on a beach in Puerto Rico

Weddings

Valerie Bertinelli,
Monaco's Prince Albert,
Kim Kardashian and more join
the 2011 "I do" crew

Shania Twain
&
Frédéric Thiébaud

January 1, 2011 ■ *RINCO, PUERTO RICO*

IN THE END, IT WAS a fairy-tale wedding, but one with a hyper-modern twist: Instead of meeting cute, singer Shania Twain and Swiss businessman Frédéric Thiébaud originally got together simply to console each other, after discovering, in 2008, that their respective spouses were having an affair. Consolation turned, over time, into celebration: In August 2009 Twain told fans on her website that Thiébaud "understands me better than anyone." On Dec. 21, 2010, she announced their engagement—then surprised all but close friends by marrying 11 days later on a Puerto Rican beach.

"After [the officiant] said, 'You can now kiss the bride,' Fred picked her up and kissed her," said bridesmaid Stacy Smith, a longtime friend of Twain's. "He was just jumping for joy. They are so much fun together. He always refers to her as his 'sunshine.' He adores her."

Twain was escorted down the aisle by her son Eja, 9, who wore a white linen suit, just like the groom (whose daughter Johanna, 9, served as ring bearer.) After Twain, 45, and Thiébaud exchanged vows and Cartier bands, the couple and their 40 guests sang "All You Need Is Love."

■ *SMOOCH!*
"I'm so glad my mom has found someone to be happy with," said her musician son Wolfie, 19, who brought his Pomeranian to the festivities.

Valerie Bertinelli was still barefoot, in her bathrobe, padding around the patio at her Malibu home and greeting guests with bear hugs. They came for a New Year's party; to everyone's delight, they got a wedding instead.

"We wanted it to be a surprise," says Bertinelli, who exchanged "I do's" with her boyfriend of six years, mutual fund manager Tom Vitale, 49. "We didn't want anyone bringing presents!"

Some 100 guests, including Bertinelli's ex, rocker Eddie Van Halen, applauded after the couple took their vows under an archway of flowers overlooking the Pacific. "I do not know how to describe how I felt when she walked down the aisle," said Vitale. "It just felt completely, totally right." Why now, after six years together? "I could have spent the rest of my life with Tom and not be married," said Bertinelli, "but I wanted to call him 'my husband.'"

■ *BEACH-SIDE STYLE*
Bertinelli chose to make her day both casual and pretty. She started the morning with a flax-seed waffle, ran 2 1/2 miles on the treadmill and gave herself a quick tan-from-a-can before greeting guests, still in her bathrobe.

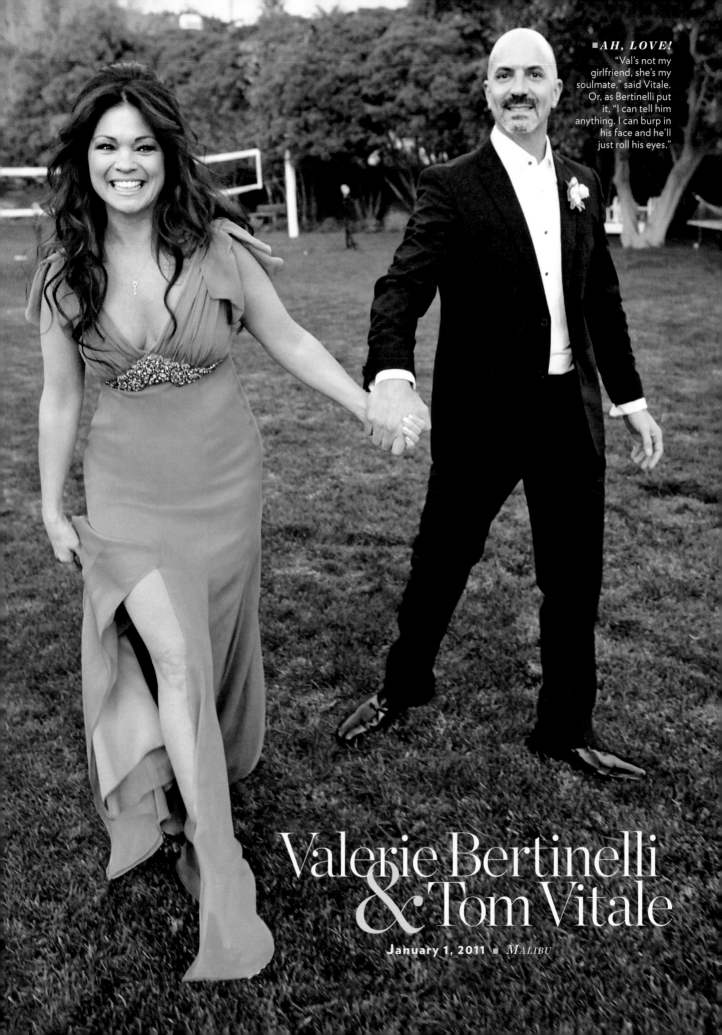

Valerie Bertinelli & Tom Vitale

January 1, 2011 ■ *MALIBU*

Kellie Pickler
&
Kyle Jacobs

January 1, 2011 ■ *Jumby Bay, Antigua*

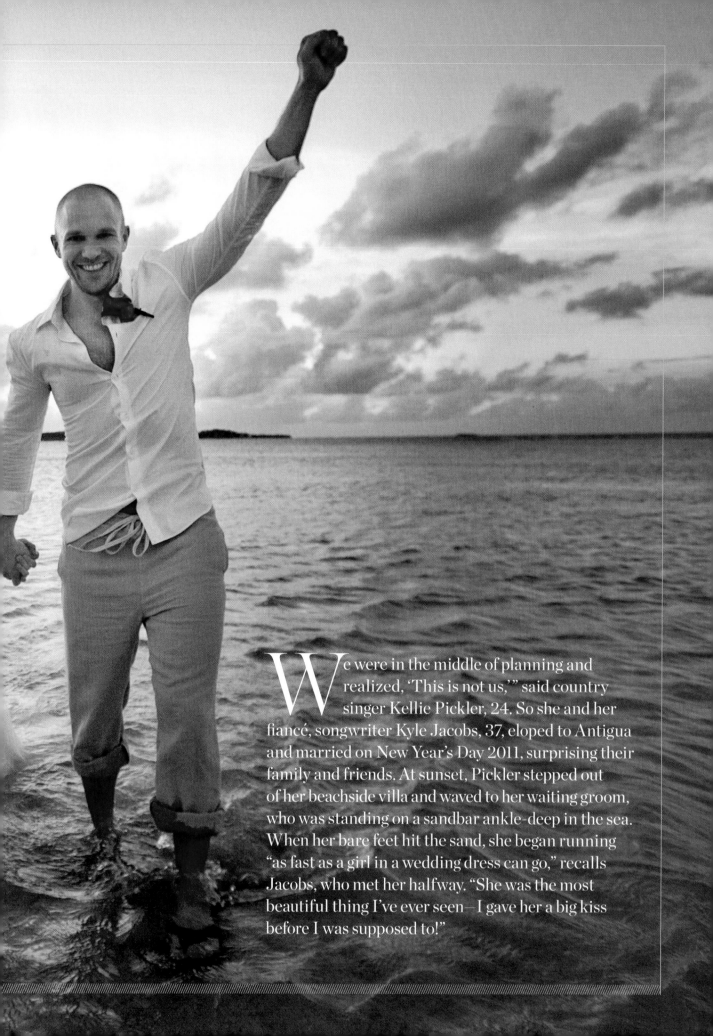

"We were in the middle of planning and realized, 'This is not us,'" said country singer Kellie Pickler, 24. So she and her fiancé, songwriter Kyle Jacobs, 37, eloped to Antigua and married on New Year's Day 2011, surprising their family and friends. At sunset, Pickler stepped out of her beachside villa and waved to her waiting groom, who was standing on a sandbar ankle-deep in the sea. When her bare feet hit the sand, she began running "as fast as a girl in a wedding dress can go," recalls Jacobs, who met her halfway. "She was the most beautiful thing I've ever seen—I gave her a big kiss before I was supposed to!"

Miranda Lambert & Blake Shelton

May 14, 2011 ▪ *BOERNE, TEXAS*

The newlyweds "were just giddy," said a guest. "She was like, 'We did it! We did it! Tell me, was it perfect?' And he said, 'Honey, it was perfect!'"

B est wedding ever ever ever," singer Ashley Monroe tweeted about the redneck-chic nuptials, at a ranch outside San Antonio, Texas, of two of country's hottest stars. The groom wore Wranglers; the bride, who lit up the room in her mother's 1979 Gunne Sax wedding dress, was preceded down the aisle by her three dogs, done up with rhinestone collars. When the pastor told Blake, an avid outdoorsman, that he would "need to place [his bride] above hunting," recalled Lambert's mom, Bev, "Blake just gave him a look and hung his head down. It was classic Blake and people had a chance to laugh." Following the ceremony, 560 guests, among them Martina McBride, Kelly Clarkson, Trace Adkins, Reba McEntire and the members of Lady Antebellum, feasted on venison—Lambert, 27, and Shelton, 34, bagged the deer themselves—drank prickly-pear margaritas and partied into the wee hours in a converted barn. "You're going to have to excuse my Texas slang," said Bev, "but people danced their asses off!"

Charlene Wittstock & Prince Albert II

July 2, 2011 ▪ *PRINCIPALITY OF MONACO*

"I'm still under the spell of it," said a guest. "I'm happy for my prince and princess"

THE LAST TIME THE ROYAL RULER of Monaco said "I do" to a commoner, a worldwide television audience swooned, and the nuptials—of Philly-bred screen star Grace Kelly and Prince Ranier III—were hailed as the wedding of the century. Fifty-five years later tabloid headlines dogged their son and heir, Prince Albert II, 53, as he wed South African Olympian—and Princess Grace look-alike—Charlene Wittstock, 33, in a lavish, $65 million royal marriage celebration. Albert, who has admitted fathering two children with two different women in the past, battled rumors that he had also fathered a third—after he began his relationship with Wittstock. Monaco's Palace guard strongly denied all the tales, and the newly minted Princess bride vowed to fight them lest they smudge her storybook romance. "Every morning," said the champion swimmer, "I dived into a freezing cold pool; this challenge is no more daunting."

Zara Phillips & Michael Tindall

July 30, 2011 ■ *EDINBURGH, SCOTLAND*

Festivities were held on the royal yacht *Britannia* and at the Queen's castle in Scotland

THERE WAS SOMETHING OF A FUSS the last time one of the Queen's grandkids got hitched. But three months after Hurricane Will & Kate, Zara Phillips, 30, the eldest of Queen Elizabeth's eight grandchildren, married to little fanfare, even though her groom, Mike Tindall, 32, represents British royalty of a different kind: He's captain of England's national rugby team. Though an accomplished Olympics-level equestrian, Phillips once had a penchant for body piercings and nightclubbing that caused Fleet Street to brand her the "royal rebel." For her wedding she wore a very proper Stewart Parvin gown and a tiara that was the real deal—she borrowed it from her mother, Princess Anne.

America the beautiful "took our breath away," Vanessa Williams tweeted

The bride's hapless, tinsel-toothed former alterego was a no-show. And all thought of ugly pantsuits was banished when the lady named after the land we love wowed the United Costars of America—Blake Lively, Amber Tamblyn and Alexis Bledel, her castmates from *Sisterhood of the Traveling Pants*; and Vanessa Williams and Rebecca Romijn of *Ugly Betty* fame— in a gown by Amsale's Christos label and Fred Leighton earrings, and clutching a bouquet of crimson roses. Also among the bedazzled was the one-score-and-seven-year-old bride's betrothed. The two met as film school classmates at the University of Southern California where Williams, now 30 and an indie director, showed an eye for promising talent by casting his future bride in a student film.

America Ferrera
&
Ryan Piers Williams

June 27, 2011 ■ CHAPPAQUA, N.Y.

Nicole Richie
&
Joel Madden

December 11, 2011 ■ *LOS ANGELES*

"It was magical," beamed the bride

The elephant in the room was, well, an elephant. Lionel Richie rented the behemoth for his daughter Nicole because she always dreamed—doesn't everyone?—of having a pachyderm present on her wedding day. Another double take was in store for guests as the couple were joined in matrimony by a familiar looking cleric: none other than Joseph Simmons a.k.a. Rev. Run of Run-DMC.

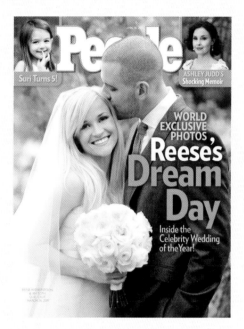

Reese Witherspoon & Jim Toth

March 26, 2011 ■ *OJAI, CALIF.*

"It was such a relaxing, beautiful, soulful night," said a friend

WHEN THE BRIDE IS AN OSCAR winner and the wedding guests include attention-getters Scarlett Johansson and her date, Sean Penn; Gwyneth Paltrow and rock star hubby Chris Martin; Kate Hudson, Alyssa Milano, Renée Zellweger, Matthew McConaughey and Borat himself, Sacha Baron Cohen, it's tough to turn heads. But it was a couple of little-known members of the wedding party who stood out in the crowd: 11-year-old maid-of-honor Ava and 7-year-old ring bearer Deacon, Witherspoon's children with ex-husband Ryan Phillippe. "They were super excited to be a part of their mom's day," said one of the guests gathered at Witherspoon's seven-acre Libbey Ranch, a rustic-chic getaway where the Tennessee-born bride keeps horses, goats, pigs and chickens, and enjoys downtime with Toth and her kids. "It was always Reese and Jim and Ava and Deacon," noted another guest. "The kids were included in everything."

■ *FATHER OF THE BRIDE* "You always dream your daughter will meet her Prince Charming, and then this guy shows up with tattoos," Lionel Richie told guests of his first meeting Madden, the heavily inked frontman of the band Good Charlotte. But, despite the tats, Madden had his bride's dad at "Hello": "He said Nicole and I were made for each other—that I was her Prince Charming."

LeAnn Rimes
&
Eddie Cibrian

April 22, 2011 ■ *MALIBU*

Happy to trade the scandal that engulfed them two years before the wedding bands, the country star and her dashing Cuban American beau celebrated their union with an emotional ceremony and reception among a small gathering of family and friends. "We've overcome just about everything we possibly could to be together," said Rimes, 28, who was still married to her first husband, Dean Sheremet, when she began a widely publicized romance with Cibrian, 38, her on- and off-screen love interest in *Northern Lights,* a made-for-TV Nora Roberts romantic thriller that aired on Lifetime in 2009. That year Cibrian divorced his wife of eight years, the mother of his two sons, to be with Rimes, whose own divorce became final in 2010. Cibrian's boys, Mason, 7, and Jake, 4, shared center stage at their dad's wedding, giving him away at the altar. Later the tykes were introduced, along with the bride and groom, "as the Cibrian family," said Rimes. "We'll always remember this day, how happy we were and how much support our family and friends gave us through a crazy, crazy time in our lives. Here's to new beginnings."

Nick Lachey
& Vanessa Minnillo

July 15, 2011 ▪ *NECKER ISLAND, B.V.I.*

"We toyed with the idea of having a big ceremony," said the groom, "and felt it just wasn't our style"

FORMER BOY-BAND heartthrob Nick Lachey and girlfriend Vanessa Minnillo, who began dating in the midst of the tabloid frenzy that accompanied his 2006 divorce from Jessica Simpson, went a long way to keep the circus at bay on their own wedding day. Guests were told only that they were to be flown to an undisclosed location and to bring their passports. The mystery locale proved to be Sir Richard Branson's private Caribbean island, where Lachey, 37, and Minnillo, 30, in a Monique Lhuillier gown, were wed in the mogul's mountaintop home. Said Lachey of the "intensely beautiful" ceremony: "It literally took my breath away."

Splits

J.Lo and Marc lead
a surprising parade of
the suddenly uncoupled

Jennifer Lopez & Marc Anthony

A couple of showbiz pros put up a great front, until they couldn't

HOT AS THEIR WILDLY SEXY PERFORMANCE looked during last spring's *American Idol* finale, their marriage had gone old. By summer it was kaput. On July 15, J.Lo and her salsa-king hubby of seven years announced to PEOPLE that they were calling it quits. During months of "nonstop arguing," said a source, "Jennifer started to kick Marc out of their house, and he'd stay for days at a time at a hotel. When he would yell, she would shut down." The news shocked fans, who saw them as the blissful parents of 3-year-old twins Max and Emme and as a loving couple who lived quietly if splendidly in suburban Brookville on Long Island, where Jenny from the block seemed very much the happy housefrau. In reality the couple were plagued by professional jealousies and rumors of infidelity. Despite the fireworks, the couple told PEOPLE they were headed to a battle-free divorce: "We have come to an amicable conclusion on all matters." Regarding finances, "they just decided to keep what belonged to each," said a friend.

George Clooney & Elisabetta Canalis

CANALIS, 33, AN ITALIAN TV hostess, was first spotted riding pillion on Clooney's motorcycle in 2009. Soon she was with him at the Oscars, Emmys and even a trip to his folks' Kentucky home. But after two years she joined the *ciao* line. "Being a long-term couple isn't really his thing," said a source. "George likes being independent." Canalis went on to *Dancing with the Stars*; Clooney began dating former WWE wrestler Stacy Keibler, 32.

Justin Timberlake & Jessica Biel

THE COUPLE ANNOUNCED their split after nearly four years—which didn't surprise some friends. "Their entire relationship, once they got past the honeymoon stage, was a roller coaster of ups and downs," said one. And might still be: By year's end the pair were being spotted together, again.

Kim Kardashian & Kris Humphries

Romance or *faux*mance? Kim Kardashian's quickie marriage leaves some fans feeling flim-flammed

A QUESTION FOR THE MODERN AGE: If you file for divorce before the E! reality show about your nuptials, *Kim's Fairytale Wedding: A Kardashian Event*, has finished airing in reruns, are you obligated to return your $2 million engagement ring? How about all those fabulous (and expensive) gifts?

Such trying issues were brought to the fore when Kim Kardashian, 31, to the surprise of some—including, to hear him tell it, her groom, 6'9" NBA star Kris Humphries, 26—filed for divorce a mere 72 days after saying "I do." It had all started with such promise, or at least great TV: The couple, who dated for six months, said the right things (He: "Within a month of meeting her I knew she was 'The One'; She: "The sexiest thing about Kris is—gosh, there are so many. It's hard to think of one"); got engaged and posed with glitter-covered miniature horses (who doesn't?); and capped it off with a blinged-out $6 million, Wolfgang Puck–catered wedding in which the bride wore three Vera Wang gowns and $15 million in jewelry. "It was like we were in heaven," said Kim.

And then? "They got engaged before ever spending a full week living together," offered a Kardashian friend. Apparently, familiarity—especially when, for the sake of the Kardashian's ongoing TV show, it occurred in the confines of a Manhattan apartment shared with Kim's sister Kourtney and boyfriend Scott—bred discontent.

Come the divorce announcement, cynics groaned. Kim's mom, Kris Jenner, asked for understanding: "She's not the first person in the world to get a divorce … people have to stop judging." Alas, many did not: The *Hollywood Reporter* speculated that the romance and wedding were "one big hoax all along" (E! denied it), and online comments about the split were often blistering.

Still, with the wedding story line gone, the divorce fallout may well provide the Kardashians with their next ratings boost. Time will tell. As for that $2 million, 20.5-carat ring? At press time, a source close to the star said Kim planned to keep it, noting, "It's a sentimental thing she'll always have."

▪ *SPIN CYCLE*
Two on the aisle, Aug. 20 (right); so in love, on *Today* (Oct. 4, top); and Mr. Humphries on the move (Oct. 20, New York City, above).

LOVE, ACTUALLY?

Bentley wanted "to really hurt me and he did," said Hebert. She bounced back strong and found love with J.P. Rosenbaum (right).

THE EVIL ONE

A Salt Lake City-area businessman and father, Williams (above) reveled in leading Hebert on: "I played everyone," he boasted. "That's never been done before."

STRIKE TWO!

In *The Bachelor*'s 2007 season, Brad Womack didn't find love and walked away from both finalists. This time, he proposed to Emily Maynard—who later broke it off.

Love, Lies and Ratings

Suppose you developed a bit of a crush on Satan? That's pretty much what happened to *The Bachelorette*'s Ashley Hebert, 27, who was falling for Bentley Williams, 29, of whom she said, "My heart races when I'm with him. …I could trust him forever."

Alas, at that point, she had no idea of the truly nasty things he'd been saying behind her back (and into the camera), including, "Ashley kind of looks like an ugly duckling," "I'm not going to pass up an opportunity to mess with her head," and, unforgettably, "I'd rather be swimming in pee than plan a wedding with Ashley." Fortunately, Bentley withdrew from the show, and Hebert found love, and became engaged to, New York construction manager J. P. Rosenbaum, 34.

Over on *The Bachelor,* the fireworks came at the end. Brad Womack dropped to one knee and proposed to Emily Maynard; cue violins! For, oh, maybe five months; Maynard had second thoughts, and the pair broke up in June.

Ashlee Simpson & Pete Wentz

The singer and her Fall Out Boy husband fall out of love

SO MUCH HAD SEEMED SO AWESOME. "He has an awesome personality," Simpson, 26, had said of her husband, Fall Out Boy bassist Pete Wentz, 31, in 2008. "There was just like this awesome connection we had." He felt the same: "It's crazy to be able to kiss your best friend," Wentz had said of their love. "It's just a really awesome thing." The 2008 wedding, too, probably merited the same teen rating: Simpson's father, Joe, a minister, conducted the ceremony in the family home, bedecked with 10,000 roses, and a bulldog named Hemingway brought the rings up the aisle. Seven months later the couple had a son, Bronx Mowgli. But last February, Simpson filed for divorce, seeking custody and spousal support. "It was a classic case," a source told PEOPLE, "of marrying young, having a kid young and growing apart over the years."

Scarlett Johansson & Ryan Reynolds

Two superheroes of hotness part company as passions cool

Breaking up is hard to do. But it can also be done with grace, as demonstrated by the 26-year-old *The Avengers* star and her Sexiest Man Alive husband. "We entered into our relationship with love," they said in a joint statement, "and it's with love and kindness we leave it."

By all accounts the couple, whose divorce became official in July, had married in a fever three years before, but their passion was overcome by the demands of dual careers that found them on distant movie sets throughout much of their time together. Their eight-year age difference and divergent personalities may also have played a role. "She's kind of dark and brooding, and he's very stable," said a pal of Reynolds', 34. Johansson was only 23 when she wed, pointed out a friend, noting at that age, "you don't know your place in life yet. He's in a different place. This was a simple mistake." Despite gossip, "There's no drama, no cheating," a friend said. "These are just two people who love each other who are not going to be together anymore."

Jesse James & Kat Von D

A future together, writ in disappearing ink

TATTOOS ARE FOREVER. But wedding plans are not so indelible. James, 42, and fiancée Von D, 29, announced their engagement in January, only to call it off via Twitter in July and renew it in August, hours after Von D's TLC tat show, *LA Ink*, was canceled. Emoticons glowed briefly, but the couple, feeling the strains of long distance commuting (he lives in Austin, she in L.A.), broke it off once again. The news spread when a blunt post appeared on Von D's Facebook page: "I am not in a relationship. And I apologize for all the 'back and forth' if it's caused any confusion."

Babies

Celebs from Neil Patrick Harris to
Alicia Silverstone welcome
a bumper crop of newcomers

Pink & Carey Hart

WILLOW SAGE ■ **June 2, 2011**

PINK HAS DELIVERED pitch-perfect performances even while hanging
upside-down from the rafters—and she hoped giving birth
to her first child would be another precisely choreographed experience.
"I was really looking forward to the whole rite of passage—giving birth
perfectly present, unmedicated, in the way nature intended," said the
singer, 31, who, with her husband, motocross champ Corey Hart, 35,
spent months planning a home birth with midwives. But when she
went into labor, her baby was in a frank-breech (head up, piked legs)
position and couldn't be flipped, so she ended up having a C-section at
the hospital. "Turns out this little girl had other plans," says the pop
star. "She is my daughter after all."

Since arriving on June 2, Willow Sage has been a little more
cooperative. "Everyone gives you this terrifying picture of no sleep
at all, bickering," says the Grammy winner. "They make it sound like
waterboarding. It's not that bad." Though she admits to "one major
meltdown" their first night home: "Carey couldn't figure out who to
comfort first. It was pretty funny, actually. Poor guy."

> "I'VE HAD UPS, I'VE HAD DOWNS, BUT NOW, **I'M JUST HAPPY.** I'M HAPPY BECAUSE **I HAVE HER.** I'M HAPPY THAT I GET TO **BE HERE FOR HER**"

Christina Applegate & Martyn LeNoble

SADIE GRACE ■ **January 27, 2011**

Even as she neared her 18th hour of labor on Jan. 27, Christina Applegate remained focused. Self-conscious about her chest since being diagnosed with breast cancer in 2008 and opting for a double mastectomy, she had kept her hospital gown securely fastened. "I don't let anyone see my top half," says the actress, who has undergone reconstructive surgery. "That whole area has remained very private."

That changed the moment Sadie Grace, her daughter with musician-fiancé Martyn LeNoble, 41, was born. Applegate, 39, let her gown fall off as the nurses placed her baby on her chest. "It was such a liberating and beautiful moment," she says. "I didn't care. It didn't matter anymore. Not only was she the most beautiful thing that's ever happened to me—but she saved me too. I got to abandon resentments that I've held on to in that vicinity for years because [my chest] is where she feels the most comfortable and where she's the happiest."

Neil Patrick Harris
& David Burtka

HARPER GRACE ■ *GIDEON SCOTT* ■ **October 12, 2011**

***HOW I MET YOUR MOTHER*'S NEIL PATRICK HARRIS**
and partner David Burtka waited seven years, "until the
timing was right," says the actor, to become parents.
"I always thought I'd make a good parent, but I was
single and led a solitary life for many, many years," says
Harris, 38. "Then I met David, and he had experience
with kids and wanted to have a family too." The couple
found an egg donor anonymously and "an amazing
surrogate who had helped a same-sex couple before.
And then we inserted two eggs, one with my sperm,
one with David's sperm, and they both took." Says
Burtka: "When we first found out it was fraternal twins,
we were thrilled. We don't know whose is whose, but
it's amazing how different they already are. She is
all girl, and he is all boy." Both parents are blissfully
happy and have no doubt that all the challenges
were worth it. "Same-sex parenthood doesn't happen
accidentally," notes Harris. "You have to really want it."

Alicia Silverstone & Christopher Jarecki

BEAR BLU ▪ May 5, 2011

"WE ARE ALL THREE IN LOVE," the actress blogged soon after she and her husband, Christopher Jarecki, welcomed son Bear Blu, 7 lbs. 15 oz., to the world. "I'm so grateful to this community for all the love, support, good wishes and happy vibes you've sent me during my pregnancy … it has been wonderful. Thank you all!"

Silverstone, 34, who recently wrote a vegan cookbook, *The Kind Diet,* and Jarecki, 40, a rock musician, wed in 2005 after eight years together.

Kase Townes Murray made his debut on July 11, weighing in at 7 lbs. 6 oz. "We have parent goggles; we think he's perfect," says new mom Jewel, whose son's name combined that of a close friend of her husband, bull rider Ty Murray, 41, and one of Jewel's favorite singer-songwriters, Townes Van Zandt. "He's mellow and chill."

The couple plan to raise Kase on their Stephenville, Texas, ranch, where Ty— a fifth-generation cowboy— tends to cattle and horses. "I can't wait until Kase goes out there with me," says Ty. But how long before Kase mounts a bull himself? "I don't want him to ride," admits Ty. "It is the most dangerous job in the world. But if he's as crazy as I was about it, then what do you do? One of our biggest dreams for Kase is that he finds something he loves." Adds Jewel: "We want him to find his passion. Whatever that is, we are fine with it." She pauses, then laughs. "But I *hope* it isn't bull-riding."

Jewel & Ty Murray

KASE TOWNES ■ **July 11, 2011**

Mariah Carey & Nick Cannon

MOROCCAN AND MONROE

April 30, 2011

After a difficult pregnancy, Mariah Carey savors each milestone with her twins, son Moroccan ("Roc") and daughter Monroe ("Roe"). "I'm blessed," she told ABC's Barbara Walters, "and so thankful." Dad calls his girl Little Diva because "she's spicy, like her mom." His boy, he says, noting that vaccine shots didn't faze him, "is tough—Roc's a perfect name for him. My son is like Superman; he's trying to pull himself up and crawl." (Perhaps unlike Superman, though, he giggles "when you blow on his stomach.") Keeping with the superhero theme, the family dressed up as the Incredibles for Halloween.

Elton John & David Furnish

ZACHARY JACKSON LEVON ■ **December 25, 2010**

TALK ABOUT CHRISTMAS GIFTS: Zachary Jackson Levon, singer Elton John and partner David Furnish's first child, was born via a surrogate in California on Dec. 25. So far, so normal: "I'm like a gibbering wreck in front of him," Elton John told British TV two months into fatherhood. "I make up songs and sing to him in gibberish."

Cynthia Nixon & Christine Marinoni

MAX ELLINGTON ▪ **February 7, 2011**

NIXON, 44, and her fiancée, stay-at-home mom Marinoni, 43, welcomed their first child together on Feb. 7. Marinoni, who started dating the *Sex and the City* star in 2004, gave birth to son Max in New York City. Nixon has two children, Samantha, 14, and Charles, 8, from her relationship with Danny Mozes.

Six months after Mariska Hargitay and her husband, Peter Hermann, 43, adopted their daughter Amaya (right, below), everybody was just getting into the swing of things. "We were just figuring out what she likes and doesn't like," Hargitay says. A nursery was up and running on the set of Mom's hit show *Law & Order: Special Victims Unit.* And, given their lengthy wait before the adoption of Amaya had come through, the couple had already started the process once more so that Amaya and her older brother August, 5, would get a baby brother or sister in the next few years.

And then: Things happened, fast. Days after their paperwork was processed, Hargitay, 47, got the startling and delightful news that they'd be getting a baby boy (it helped a lot that they had already been vetted). They brought Andrew Nicolas Hargitay Hermann to their New York City home days later. "Everything," she says, "felt divinely right."

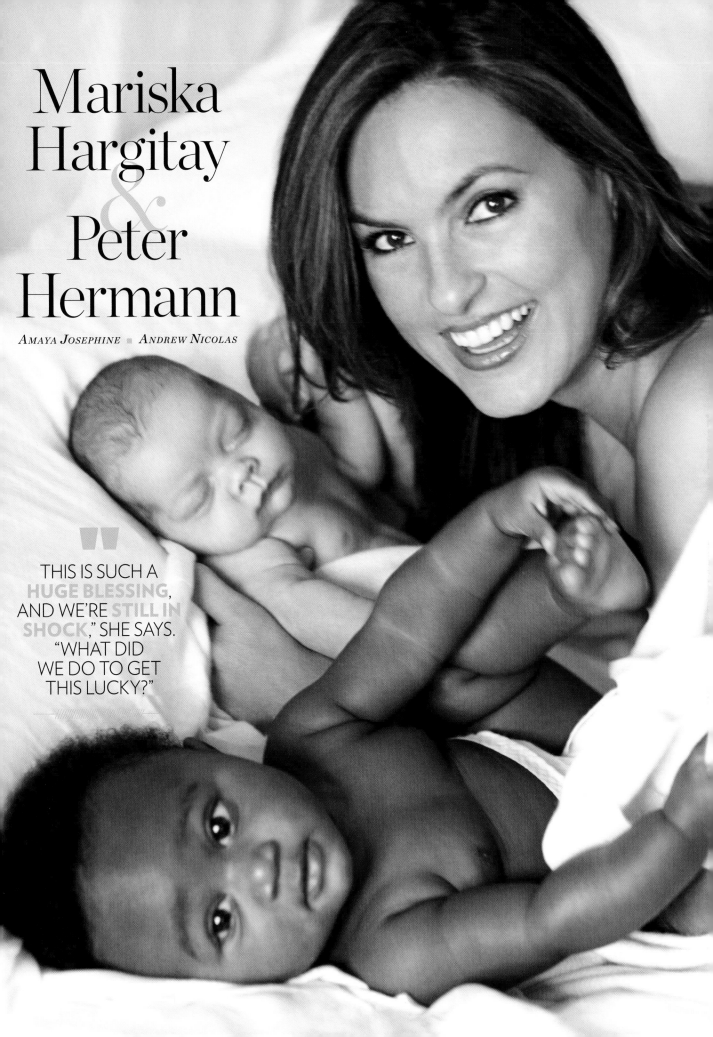

Mariska Hargitay & Peter Hermann

Amaya Josephine ■ *Andrew Nicolas*

" THIS IS SUCH A **HUGE BLESSING**, AND WE'RE **STILL IN SHOCK**," SHE SAYS. "WHAT DID WE DO TO GET THIS LUCKY?"

Alanis Morrisette & Mario Treadway

EVER IRME ▪ **December 25, 2010**

Alanis Morissette, 36, and her husband, Mario "Souleye" Treadway, 30, got the best Christmas gift ever when their first child—a boy they named Ever—was born on Dec. 25. The multiple-Grammy winner, who was previously engaged to fellow Canadian Ryan Reynolds, married her rapper spouse last May.

Owen Wilson & Jade Duell

ROBERT FORD ▪ **January 14, 2011**

The *Midnight in Paris* star sees the world from a blurry new perspective since he and his girlfriend, 29, welcomed their little Focker in Hawaii. "You look at every place as a potential nap place," Wilson told Jay Leno on *The Tonight Show.* "You've got to look for your chances to catch up."

Nicole Kidman & Keith Urban

FAITH MARGARET   **December 28, 2010**

TALK ABOUT SURPRISES:
In January, Nicole Kidman, 43, and Keith Urban revealed that, three weeks earlier, they had welcomed a daughter, Faith Margaret, born to a surrogate. "No words can adequately convey the incredible gratitude that we feel for everyone who was so supportive throughout this process," the couple, clearly elated, said in a statement, "in particular our gestational carrier."

■ **HARRY CARRY**
Helped by his young costars and a *Who's Who* cast of Britain's best, Daniel Radcliffe, now 22, carried eight Potter films (and, in *Deathly Hallows*, actor Warwick Davis).

Movies

Harry Potter

Deathly Hallows — Part 2 brings the films to a satisfying end, but the magic lingers on

WHEN THEY SHOT THE VERY FIRST SCENE in 2000—for *Harry Potter and the Sorcerer's Stone*—everyone was nervous. "To be 'special' just because I had been picked for this part," recalled Daniel Radcliffe, then 11, of being stared at by 150 extras dressed in Hogwarts uniforms, "was . . . bizarre."

So, a bit, was the challenge of directing preteens:"We couldn't [keep the camera] on the actors for a long time because in the very next frame they could be looking directly into the camera or giggling." director Chris Columbus told ENTERTAINMENT WEEKLY. Then came The Moment: After repeated takes of the movie's final scene, where Harry prepares to board the Hogwarts Express back to the real world, Radcliffe asked to give his own reading of the line "I'm not going home. Not really." Seeing that take the next day "was electrifying," says Columbus. "With one line, Dan managed to convey the haunting complexity we had been looking for. I turned to our producer. There were tears in his eyes.... We knew, at that moment, that we had cast the right actor." For 10 years and 8 movies, Radcliffe, together with Emily Watson and Rupert Grint, made Potter magical. The final film, *Harry Potter and the Deathly Hallows: Part 2*, released in July, earned over $1.3 billion and had the biggest weekend opening in history.

■ *A-WIZARDING THEY WENT*
The splendidly named Rupert Grint, then 14 (left); Radcliffe, 13; and Emma Watson, 12; during the second Potter movie, 2002's *Chamber of Secrets*. For the future, says Radcliffe, "I'd like to work on smaller things for awhile. At 5'5", I am not a natural action-movie star. Lucky for me, I've already done enough stunts to last a lifetime."

■ **HUNGOVER**
Crystal the capuchin monkey gracefully shared screen time with (from left) Ed Helms, Bradley Cooper and Zach Galifianakis.

The Hangover Part II
VS. Bridemaids

FINGER AMPUTATION, face tattoo and a smoking monkey? Or projectile vomiting in a bridal dress shop? Two films about premarital mayhem—one each from the male and female point of view—provided plenty of material for nuanced debate about artistic merit. *Hangover* made more money ($581 million vs. $286) but *Bridesmaids*, cowritten by and starring Kristen Wiig, got better reviews and made her a very hot Hollywood property.

■ **WIIGING OUT**
Saturday Night Live star Wiig (above, left) cowrote herself a huge career boost.

■ **NOT SO MUCH GREEN**
The Green Lantern, Ryan Reynold's highly hyped action debut, went belly-up.

Bombs Away!

BAD MOVIES ARE A DIME a dozen; to truly bomb, you need to spend zillions, market relentlessly, and *then* flop. Some expensive flicks that went kerflooey in 2011: *Sucker Punch* (cost: $82 million; domestic box office: $36 million); *Mars Needs Moms* (cost: $150 million; box office: $21 million) *Arthur* (cost: $40 million; box office: $33 million) and *The Beaver,* starring Mel Gibson (cost: $21 million; box office: $970,800).

Transformers

IN A SUBTLE AND moving character study that rivals anything Ingmar Bergman ever made . . . okay, no. Let's try again: In a colossal display of the power of CGI and the joy of watching massive metal doing the monster mash, *Transformers: Dark of the Moon* (starring Shia LaBeouf and Rosie Huntington-Whiteley, above) earned over $350 million in the U.S., making it the second-highest grossing movie of the year.

■ *AU REVOIR?* Pole-axed by Paris, Owen Wilson falls in love; his fiancée (Rachel McAdams) misses Malibu.

Midnight in Paris

FORTY-ONE FILMS IN, director Woody Allen, 75, had the highest-earning movie of his career with a whimsical meditation on love, dreams, Paris and the seductive delights—and dangers—of nostalgia. "I'm wearying of movies that are for 'everybody'— which means, nobody in particular," wrote Roger Ebert. "*Midnight in Paris* is for me, in particular, and that's just fine with moi."

AMERICAN ENTERPRISE
Ryan Seacrest, Jennifer Lopez, Steven Tyler and original judge Randy Jackson.

TV

The rebooted *Idol* was something to sing about, and Susan Lucci ran out of soap

■ *EX FACTOR*
Simon Cowell reteamed with former *Idol* colleague Paula Adbul.

Idol Comeback

The startling and jubilant resuscitation of FOX's *American Idol* can best be summed up by a quote from new judge and rock legend Steven Tyler: "Slap that baby on the ass and call me Christmas!" Tyler, who woke up fans of the aging reality behemoth with his zesty, unpredictable outrageousness, was new to the judges' panel, along with superstar Jennifer Lopez: Dressed beautifully and weeping like an Oscar winner when singers triumphed or failed, she too was an unexpected gift to the show. Suddenly no one worried that *Idol* couldn't survive without its greatest asset, the adroitly sarcastic Simon Cowell, who left at the end of season 9.

Cowell, though, was in the wings, preparing to return to FOX with an Americanized version of his jumbo British hit *The X Factor*. Expectations were huge—he was even bringing along his former *Idol* Sancho Panza, Paula Abdul—and Cowell coolly predicted a debut audience of 20 million. Anything less, he said, would be "a disappointment." Well, he was disappointed, but the show was by no means a flop. "Now I'm kind of back in the real world," said Cowell, "and I'm seeing this grow naturally."

The Kennedys

▪ **THE NEW FRONTIER** The show's actual broadcast was less controversial than its initial cancellation, but Barry Pepper (right, with Greg Kinnear as Jack and Katie Holmes as Jackie) won an Emmy playing Robert.

ALTHOUGH NO KENNEDYS are currently in office, the Camelot saga remains one hot politico-potato. *The Kennedys,* an 8-hour miniseries focusing on John, Robert and paterfamilias Joe, was dumped by the History Channel after experts who'd read scripts claimed it was inaccurate. Caroline Kennedy's displeasure reportedly also played a part. The show, which ultimately aired on ReelzChannel, was definitely the least reverential TV portrayal ever of the dynasty— it even included the lobotomy of Rosemary Kennedy.

A Computer Wins *Jeopardy!*

Artificial intelligence has mastered the game show: Watson, an IBM supercomputer, beat *Jeopardy* champs Ken Jennings and Brad Rutter. A humbled Jennings paraphrased *The Simpsons*: "I, for one, welcome our new computer overlords."

All My Children

AFTERNOON soap operas, their audiences fading, took one step closer to twilight Sept. 23: After 41 years, ABC's *All My Children* went off the air; soon only four network soaps will remain. So ended the adventures of Pine Valley's Erica Kane, played by icon Susan Lucci since *AMC*'s launch in 1970. There was talk of reviving the show online, but Lucci has already moved on to *Army Wives*. She takes with her 21 Emmy nominations and a single win. "It's been a fantastic journey," she said.

■ *THE LUCCI LOOK*
Hugging it out in an episode from the show's last month, and in 1970 with actor Charles Frank, who played Dr. Jeff Martin.

Ricky Gervais

It wasn't so much a roast as a flash fire: The British comedian hosted the Golden Globes and mocked one celeb after another without mercy. Introducing Robert Downey Jr., he said the star's biggest credits were stints at Betty Ford and the L.A. county jail. Buzz about the performance persisted for weeks in Hollywood, but Gervais insisted (wink, wink) it was a "gentle ribbing of the industry."

Music

Katy Perry has had such a whirlwind 2011 that even she has probably had trouble keeping track of her hair color. (If it's Tuesday, it must be . . . chartreuse?) Perry started the year with a No. 1 single, "Firework", and went on to notch two more chart toppers, "E.T." and "Last Friday Night (T.G.I.F.)" from her album *Teenage Dream*. That put her in rare company. The only other solo artist to launch five No. 1 singles off one album? Let's have a (gloved) hand for . . . Michael Jackson.

Katy Perry

KANDY-KOLORED KICKOFF
Looking like a Punk Barbi play-set come to life,
Perry & Co. launched the North American leg
of her California Dreams Tour in Duluth, Ga.

Adele

Begone, sophomore slump! A Brit dazzles the second time around

Precocious Londoner Adele set records with her 2008 debut album *19* (her age when she began recording it). Her 2011 follow-up. *21* (ditto), continued her arc of triumph, selling 10 million worldwide and counting.

Her secret? "I didn't know what to write," Adele admits. "Luckily I broke up with my ex—that's good material." Among her lessons learned: "I'd rather date an ugly, hilarious guy than Leonardo DiCaprio. Humor keeps relationships together." Though her sound can be soulful, she resists being bundled with a recent wave of British female singers, noting, "We're a gender, not a genre." -

U2 Can
Be the Best

HE PROBABLY STILL HASN'T found what he's looking for, but Bono and crew chalked up another major achievement as they continued their search: their two-year, 110-show 360° tour, made more than any rock caravan, ever–$736 million, with more than 7.2 million tickets sold.

■ *BIG BAD BONO*
The band performed on the largest rock stage-set ever produced: a 167-ft. tall sci-fi contraption nicknamed The Claw.

Jay-Z  Kanye

AFTER A YEAR OF ANTICIPATION, Kanye West and Jay-Z finally released their collaborative album, *Watch the Throne.* The pair of kings quickly ruled the charts with their combo effort—plus a little help from Mrs. Jay-Z (a.k.a. Beyoncé) and an Otis Redding sample.

■ *ROCKIN' THE MICS*
West (left) and Jay-Z hit the stage at the South by Southwest Music Festival in Austin, Tex., in March.

■ *POLE DANCER*
Gyrating and whipping her hair at the iHeartRadio Music Festival in Las Vegas.

Lady Gaga

Little Monsters everywhere clamored for *Born This Way*, which scored a No. 1 hit with the title track and sold 1.1 million copies in its first week. Amid all the crazy costumes, she collaborated with Clarence Clemons and Tony Bennett, who went, well, gaga, predicting "She will become bigger than Elvis."

BLACK & WHAT?
Making like the Flying Nun in London.

EGG-CELLENT!
Hatching her encased entrance at the Grammys.

EYELINER LOVE
Taking makeup tips from Cleopatra in New York City.

TAKE THAT, JOAN COLLINS!
Shoulder padding that a *Dynasty* diva could only dream of.

AQUA WOMAN
Corseted for the CFDA Fashion Awards.

Best *of* 2011

Hollywood, too, invests in precious metals

Looking back, there were, of course, red carpet trends: Bright colors made a comeback, and metallics—silver, gold and copper, in long, short and micro-mini—were everywhere. But, in the end, fashion is alchemy: You can follow the rules or break the rules, try hard or luck out, rise or fall on a risk. There is, in short, no guaranteed "how" to get to "wow"—yet we all know it in a blink when we see it. Here are 10 celebs who, for one night at least, found the magic formula.

■ LONG AND LEAN
Anne Hathaway, Golden Globes, Armani Privé

DIVINE DRAPE
Vanessa Hudgens,
Sucker Punch premiere,
Alberta Ferretti

**ELEGANT
FLIRT**
Emma Stone,
MTV Movie Awards,
Bottega Veneta

TULLE FANTASY
Halle Berry, Oscars, Marchesa

Best of 2011

■ SHIMMERING SLIVER
Gwyneth Paltrow, Oscars, Calvin Klein Collection

GOLD STANDARD
Heidi Klum, Grammys, Julien Macdonald

■ LADY IN RED
Sandra Bullock, Oscars, Vera Wang

VA-VA-VOOM!
Taylor Swift, *Vanity Fair*
Oscar party, Zuhair Murad

CLOUD CIRCLES
Rihanna, Grammys,
Jean Paul Gaultier

GLITTERATI
Jennifer Lopez,
Grammys, Emilio Pucci

On the *Other* Hand...

Some looks that, indeed, made people look—for maybe not entirely the right reasons

JOHNNY WEIR
Actually, we love the entire ensemble. Our only quibble is with the color of the shoelaces. Should be maybe *one* shade darker?

SHARON STONE
Of the moment? No. But channeling Mamie Eisenhower—yes!

KE$HA
The X-ray specs outfit was right for Halloween— but this was July.

KIM KARDASHIAN
Sometimes, lotsa spots is not so hots.

Cartoonish coifs
& deja vu do's

Were these celebs inspired by two-dimensional women?

■ LADY GAGA
Let's get vertical: an homage to Marge Simpson's huge hive?

■ KATY PERRY
Let's hear it for *Josie and the Pussycats* ears?

■ NICKI MINAJ
says "I do" the Bride of Frankenstein look.

■ DAVID ARQUETTE
Perfect, had he been auditioning for *Toots Barnum, the Color-Blind Carnival Barker*. Alas, no.

You Glow, Girl!

Her Oscar-hosting talents?
Up for debate, maybe.
But there's no question
Anne Hathaway, living every
woman's couture fantasy,
can flat-out wear a dress
(or pants!)

▪ In Vivienne
Westwood
Couture

▪ In Lanvin

▪ In Atelier
Versace

▪ In Tom
Ford

■ In Oscar de
la Renta

■ In Giorgio
Armani Privé

Gender-Bending Supermodels

Some mannequins began as—or still are—guys

■ **ISIS KING** returned as an *America's Next Top Model* all-star in September.

■ **ANDREJ PEJIC** was Gaultier's runway bride.

■ **LEA T.** booked Rio's fashion week.

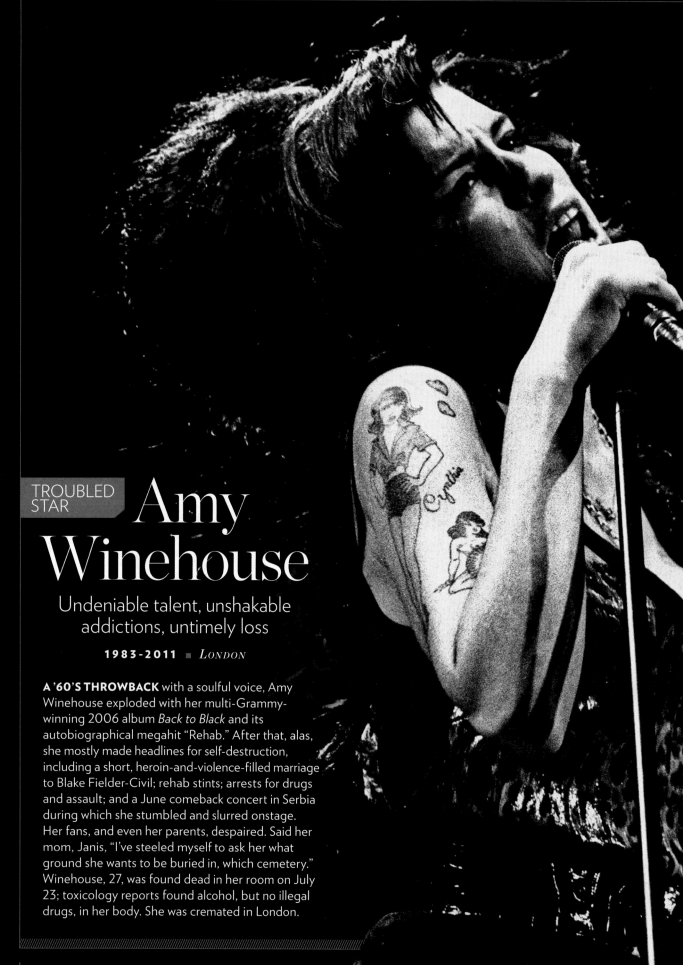

Amy Winehouse

Undeniable talent, unshakable addictions, untimely loss

1983-2011 ■ *LONDON*

A '60'S THROWBACK with a soulful voice, Amy Winehouse exploded with her multi-Grammy-winning 2006 album *Back to Black* and its autobiographical megahit "Rehab." After that, alas, she mostly made headlines for self-destruction, including a short, heroin-and-violence-filled marriage to Blake Fielder-Civil; rehab stints; arrests for drugs and assault; and a June comeback concert in Serbia during which she stumbled and slurred onstage. Her fans, and even her parents, despaired. Said her mom, Janis, "I've steeled myself to ask her what ground she wants to be buried in, which cemetery." Winehouse, 27, was found dead in her room on July 23; toxicology reports found alcohol, but no illegal drugs, in her body. She was cremated in London.

Farewell

Fans, friends and family mourn the loss of Elizabeth Edwards, *Columbo*'s Peter Falk, saxmaster Clarence Clemons, funnyman Leslie Nielsen and many more

DEATH'S HELPER

Jack Kevorkian

A controversial pathologist known as "Dr. Death"

1928-2011 ■ *ROYAL OAK, MICH.*

MY SPECIALTY," Jack Kevorkian once said, "is death." A passionate advocate for assisted suicide for terminally-ill patients who wanted to manage their own exit, he was said to have had a role in more than 130 deaths, often through the use of his Thanatron, a machine that allowed patients to self-administer lethal narcotics. In 1999, after video surfaced of him administering a deadly dose, he was convicted of second-degree murder and spent 8 years in prison. Kevorkian died—peacefully, said his daughter—at 83 of kidney-related complications, convinced to the end that history would be on his side. "It may not be in my lifetime, " he said, "but my opponents are going to lose. There's a lot of human misery out there."

Peter Falk

CLASSIC DETECTIVE

1927-2011 ■ *BEVERLY HILLS*

With a rumpled raincoat and an endearingly daft demeanor, he won four Emmys and made Columbo a detective for the ages

WHEN PETER FALK DUCKED OUT of a downpour and into a Manhattan coat shop in 1966, he was just looking to stay dry. Instead, he found the raincoat that became the trademark of Lieutenant Columbo, the rumpled, quirky TV detective he played for four decades. Falk "was Columbo," said series co-creator William Link. "He was very forgetful. He couldn't find things on set, like his keys. It was endearing." And life-changing. "He struggled with loving Columbo, but also breaking away from it," said daughter Catherine Falk. "But deep down, he enjoyed it."

A New York native, Falk, who died at 83, had worried that his glass right eye (the result of cancer at age 3) would limit his acting roles. Instead he charmed audiences on TV and in films like *The Princess Bride*. "He loved what he did and he loved life," said friend Paul Reiser. "He was a true force of nature."

Leslie Nielson

SURELY, HE JESTED

1926-2011   *FT. LAUDERDALE, FLA.*

Tutu much was barely enough for *Naked Gun's* deadpan master

Leslie Nielsen already had a successful 32-year career in stage, film and TV drama before he revealed, in his mid-50s, his true talent: deadpan comedy. His hilarious bit as a doofus doc in 1980's *Airplane!* led, eight years later, to the role he was born to play: *Naked Gun*'s immortal, clueless cop Det. Frank Drebin—the man who, when asked by a love interest if he wanted a nightcap, reliably answered, "No, thank you, I don't wear them."

The son of a Canadian Mountie, Nielsen, who died of pneumonia at 84, maintained that silly was his true self. *Gun* executive producer Jim Abrahams, concurs: Always and inevitably, says Abrahams, Nielsen "carried a fart machine in his hand. He would squeeze it and squiggle like he was uncomfortable, and everybody would be embarrassed. He was a ham."

WHITE HAT

James Arness

1923-2011 ■ *Los Angeles*

For two decades, if you fought the law in *Gunsmoke*'s Dodge City, the law won

THE REAL WORLD MIGHT COULD be going to heck, but for 20 years—still the longest run in American TV history—Marshal Matt Dillon kept the peace in Dodge City. Genial and big (6'7") but tough and quick on the draw when he had to be, Arness's iconic lawman moseyed into living rooms in 1955 and didn't ride off into the sunset until 1975. Fans relished his G-rated sexual tension with saloon keeper Miss Kitty (actress Amanda Blake, whose character, in the original radio series, took a distinctly pecuniary approach to romance) and his weekly interactions with Doc Adams (Milburn Stone), Chester (Dennis Weaver) and, for three years, Burt Reynolds as the part-Indian blacksmith Quint. Offscreen, Arness, a WWII vet who was severely wounded at Anzio and won a Bronze Star, was a twice-married father of three who had little interest in publicity; *TV Guide* once dubbed him "the Greta Garbo of Dodge City."

FILM
LEGEND

Sidney Lumet

1924-2011 ▪ *NEW YORK CITY*

D og Day Afternoon; Serpico; Network; The Verdict; 12 Angry Men; The Pawnbroker. In a rich 50-year career Lumet directed 43 films that earned 46 Oscar nominations. Many featured the New York City he loved. "If you think of New York City, especially the New York of the '70s, as a roiling cesspool of bombastic thugs and criminal cops," Richard Corliss wrote in TIME, "you probably got that view from seeing films directed by Sydney Lumet."

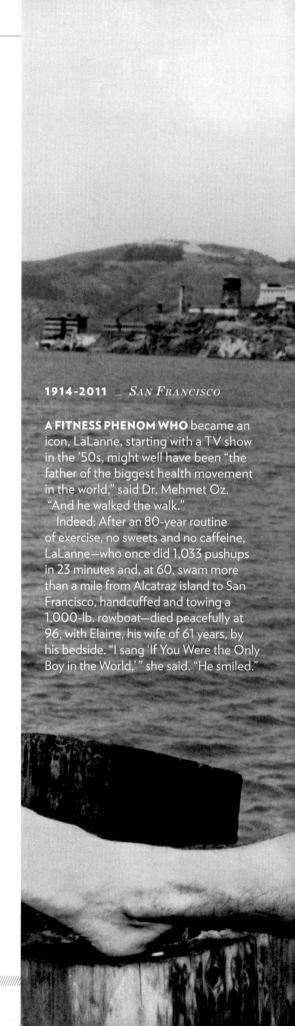

1914-2011 ▫ *SAN FRANCISCO*

A FITNESS PHENOM WHO became an icon, LaLanne, starting with a TV show in the '50s, might well have been "the father of the biggest health movement in the world," said Dr. Mehmet Oz. "And he walked the walk."

Indeed: After an 80-year routine of exercise, no sweets and no caffeine, LaLanne—who once did 1,033 pushups in 23 minutes and, at 60, swam more than a mile from Alcatraz island to San Francisco, handcuffed and towing a 1,000-lb. rowboat—died peacefully at 96, with Elaine, his wife of 61 years, by his bedside. "I sang 'If You Were the Only Boy in the World,'" she said. "He smiled."

Jack LaLane

"Inactivity is the killer," preached the exercise maven. "It's never too late"

Betty Ford

She used her bully pulpit to break boundaries and help others

1918-2011 ■ *RANCHO MIRAGE, CALIF.*

BEFORE THERE were pink ribbons, there was Betty Ford. Less than two months after Richard Nixon's resignation thrust Gerald Ford into the White House, the First Lady went public about her mastectomy—a daring move at the time.

She was only getting started. After also talking openly about her own struggle with alcohol and pills, she opened the Betty Ford Center, a drug and alcohol rehab hospital—again shedding light on a problem often left in the shadows.

Ford, who died at 93, often followed her own drummer, breaking with the GOP to support the Equal Rights Amendment and legalized abortion. On her last day in the White House, recalled photographer David Hume Kennerly, she mischievously slipped off her shoes and danced atop the Cabinet Room table.

Ryan Dunn

1977-2011 ■ *WEST GOSHEN TOWNSHIP, PA.*

An MTV star pays a terrible price for a night of drinking and bad choices

Famous for off-the-wall and gross-out stunts on MTV's *Jackass*, Ryan Dunn, 34, and his friend Zachary Hartwell, 30, died of "blunt and thermal trauma" when Dunn crashed his Porshe at an estimated 140 mph on a Pennsylvania road at 3 a.m. Authorities said toxicology tests put Dunn's blood-alcohol concentration at .196—nearly 2 1/2 times the Pennsylvania legal limit of .08.

Geraldine Ferraro

1935-2011 ■ *BOSTON*

Quietly battling cancer for
13 years, the former congresswoman
offered a profile in courage

HER RARE BLOOD cancer would give Geraldine Ferraro five years tops, doctors said in 1998. But here it was, February of year 13, and she and her best pals were gathered at her New York home. "It wasn't goodbye, but a good girlie-girl afternoon, trading stories and joking," Senator Barbara Mikulski recalled. "Her wit and grit carried her through, even in these last days."

Ferraro, a lawyer who, as a congresswoman in 1984, was tapped by Walter Mondale to be the first woman on a major presidential ticket, was 75. "She won't see the woman President who will finish breaking the glass ceiling," said Senator Kay Bailey Hutchinson, "but we will all be standing on the shoulders of Gerry Ferraro."

E-STREET
LEGEND

Clarence Clemons

For decades, the Big Man spread the joy
of sax with Springsteen's E-Street band

Jill Clayburgh

Farewell to a class act, onstage, onscreen and in real life

1944-2011 ■ *LAKEVILLE, CONN.*

"HAPPINESS," Jill Clayburgh, quoting Sigmund Freud, once told PEOPLE, "is love and work." Her dedication to the latter was never in doubt, even as she secretly struggled with chronic leukemia for 21 years, finally succumbing to the disease at 66 in the Connecticut home she shared with husband, playwright David Rabe. "Living with that for as long as she did made her appreciate things," said Jake Gyllenhaal, her costar in *Love and Other Drugs*. A theater actress who made the transition to film, Clayburgh received an Oscar nomination for 1976's *An Unmarried Woman*. Said director James L. Brooks, "Every set she was on was friendlier and warmer."

1942-2011 ■ *PALM BEACH, FLORIDA*

AS BRUCE Springsteen frequently told the story, he was playing an Asbury Park, N.J., bar on a stormy night in 1971 when the 6'4" Clarence Clemons walked in, carrying a sax, and Springsteen asked if he wanted to sit in. For the next 30 or so years, onstage and on record, in hits like "Rosalita," "Thunder Road" and "Jungleland," the Boss and the Big Man were inseparable. "He was my great friend, my partner," Springsteen said in a statement after Clemons passed away at 69 following a stroke. "With Clarence at my side, my band and I were able to tell a story far deeper than those simply contained in the music." Fans will remember Clemons as much for his benevolent spirit. "His warmth came out in his playing," said Paul Schaffer. "He was a sweet, sweet soul."

Jane Russell

The look said "come hither"; the gun said, "but be *real* careful." Such was the dicey allure of a '50s siren

SCREEN
TEMPTRESS

1921-2011 ■ *SANTA MARIA, CALIF.*

SHE WAS THE LAST of the Hollywood bombshells, with a bio that hit every note of a now-lost era. At 19, Russell was plucked from obscurity by Howard Hughes (whom she later dated) to star in a steamy western called *The Outlaw* (her cleavage caused the Hays Office to keep the film off most screens for years). During WWII, a sultry poster of Russell became a G.I. favorite; later she would costar in *Gentlemen Prefer Blondes* with Marilyn Monroe and *His Kind of Woman* with Robert Mitchum; inspire Bob Hope gags ("Culture is the ability to describe Jane Russell without moving your hands"); and have her hand- and footprints immortalized in cement outside Grauman's Chinese Theater. In the years before her death in February, at 89, Russell still occasionally sang at an airport hotel lounge in Santa Maria, Calif.

Nick Ashford

1941-2011 ▪ *New York City*

SOUL VETERAN

NEXT TIME YOU'RE SINGING, humming or dancing to the Motown classics "Ain't No Mountain High Enough," "Ain't Nothing Like the Real Thing" and "Reach Out and Touch (Somebody's Hand)" or Chaka Khan's "I'm Every Woman" have a kind thought for Nick Ashford, who cowrote those songs with his wife and musical partner, Valerie Simpson. The couple also had a memorable hit as performers with 1984's "Solid" ("Solid as a rock ... The thrill is still hot hot hot hot hot hot hot hot ...").

Ashford, 70, died of throat cancer in August.

Knut

2006-2011 ▪ *Berlin*

The Berlin Zoo's supercute cub enchanted fans around the world

CELEBRITY BEAR

AWWWW
Bottle-fed from birth by a zookeeper, Knut became an ursine icon.

Drawing millions of visitors, Knut (pronounced kuh-NOOT), the furry white superstar of the Berlin Zoo, was used to putting on a show. But the horrifying spectacle some 600 fans witnessed March 19 was no act. Playing on the rocks, Knut, 4, suddenly convulsed and plunged into the water. When the nearly 600-lb. bear stayed under, visitors realized he'd died before their eyes. (Polar bears can live more than 20 years in captivity; zoo experts initially identified certain mutations in the brain as a likely cause of death.) People around the world mourned the loss of the cuddly cub who had become a global celebrity after being rejected by his mother and lovingly bottle-fed back to health by keeper Thomas Dörflein. "Knut," said Heiner Klös, bear curator at the zoo where the polar bear helped generate millions in revenue, "brought us a lot of joy."

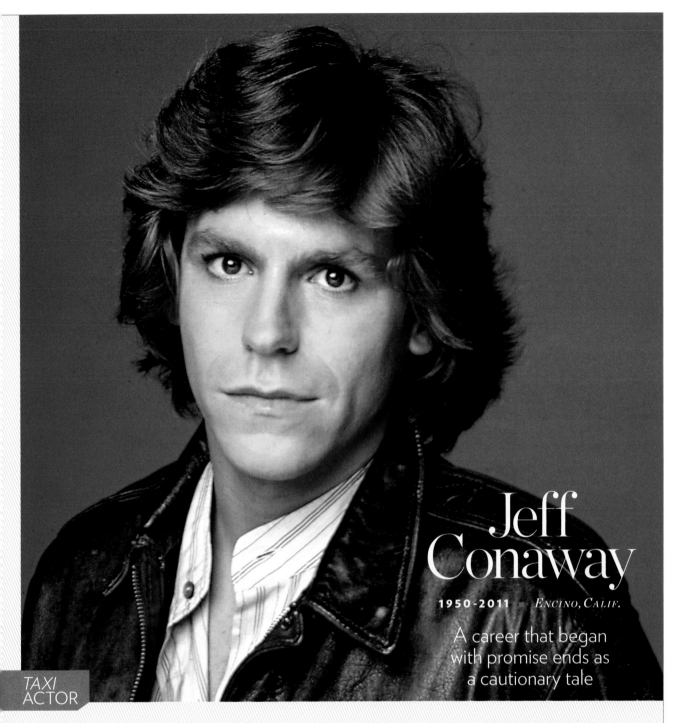

Jeff Conaway

1950-2011 · ENCINO, CALIF.

A career that began
with promise ends as
a cautionary tale

TAXI
ACTOR

"I HAD A HARD LIFE," Jeff Conaway told PEOPLE in '06 before being treated for addiction to alcohol and pain medication on the VH1 reality show *Celebrity Rehab*. In addition to his chemical dependencies, Conaway grappled with lifelong depression and memories of childhood abuse at the hands of a neighbor. "I'm not afraid [to die]," he said. "It's got to be better on the other side."

On May 27 friends got the grim news they had long feared. Conaway, 60, had died at an L.A.-area hospital, nine days after being found unconscious in his home—the apparent result of pneumonia and physical damage from prolonged drug use. He was taken off life support,

"based on advice from physicians," said his manager Phil Brock. "The situation was hopeless."

It was a bleak end for the onetime sex symbol, who starred alongside John Travolta in *Grease*, followed by the sitcom *Taxi*. When he began battling addiction, his prospects dried up. "I'm a great actor," he lamented in '06. "Nobody will give me a chance."

After rehab stints, Conaway suffered a serious setback in 2010, when an accident left him with a broken hip, arm and neck and a brain hemorrhage—exacerbating the chronic pain that first led to his addiction to pain medication. "He was a wonderful, decent man," said John Travolta. "We will miss him."

Elizabeth

CLASS
ACT

Edwards

1949-2010 ▪ *Chapel Hill, N.C.*

Faced with a cascade of misfortune, she turned her personal struggle into a life that inspired others

SHE CAME INTO PUBLIC view as a political wife; she will be remembered as every inch her own woman: a loving mom, strong in adversity, graceful even as fate dealt, it seemed, from the bottom of the deck.

As her husband, a shiny, camera-ready North Carolina senator, campaigned for the Democratic presidential nomination in 2008, Elizabeth learned the cancer she had battled three years before had returned. Nonetheless, she encouraged her husband to continue his quest.

Then came rumors that John had been having an affair with campaign videographer Rielle Hunter. At first he denied it—then admitted it was true and ended his campaign.

Hunter had given birth to a child; John at first denied he was the father—only to admit, in 2010, the infant was his.

Through it all, Elizabeth absorbed the blows and focused on one question: What could she do to ensure the happiness of her children, Cate, Jack and Emma Claire? In the end, she decided that included keeping the lines of communication open with John, who would one day be their only parent.

After fighting cancer for six years, Elizabeth died at home, surrounded by family, including John. Said Cate: "She taught me the meaning of grace."

2011

Masthead ■

EDITOR Cutler Durkee **DESIGN DIRECTOR** Andrea Dunham **DEPUTY DESIGN DIRECTOR** Dean Markadakis **PHOTO DIRECTOR** Chris Dougherty **PHOTO EDITOR** C.Tiffany Lee-Ramos **DESIGNERS** Cynthia Rhett, Margarita Mayoral, Joan Dorney **WRITERS** Steve Dougherty, Alex Tresniowski, Tom Gliatto, Chuck Arnold **REPORTER** Ellen Shapiro **COPY EDITOR** Will Becker **SCANNERS** Brien Foy, Stephen Pabarue **IMAGING** Francis Fitzgerald (Imaging Director), Rob Roszkowski (Imaging Manager), Romeo Cifelli, Charles Guardino (Imaging Production Managers), Jeff Ingledue **SPECIAL THANKS TO** Céline Wojtala, David Barbee, Jane Bealer, Patricia Clark, Margery Frohlinger, Suzy Im, Ean Sheehy, Patrick Yang

· ·

TIME HOME ENTERTAINMENT PUBLISHER Richard Fraiman **VICE PRESIDENT, BUSINESS DEVELOPMENT & STRATEGY** Steven Sandonato **EXECUTIVE DIRECTOR, MARKETING SERVICES** Carol Pittard **EXECUTIVE DIRECTOR, RETAIL & SPECIAL SALES** Tom Mifsud **EXECUTIVE DIRECTOR, NEW PRODUCT DEVELOPMENT** Peter Harper **EDITORIAL DIRECTOR** Stephen Koepp **DIRECTOR, BOOKAZINE DEVELOPMENT & MARKETING** Laura Adam **PUBLISHING DIRECTOR** Joy Butts **FINANCE DIRECTOR** Glenn Buonocore **ASSISTANT GENERAL COUNSEL** Helen Wan **ASSISTANT DIRECTOR, SPECIAL SALES** Ilene Schreider **BOOK PRODUCTION MANAGER** Suzanne Janso **DESIGN & PREPRESS MANAGER** Anne-Michelle Gallero **BRAND MANAGER** Michela Wilde **SPECIAL THANKS TO** Christine Austin, Jeremy Biloon, Jim Childs, Susan Chodakiewicz, Rose Cirrincione, Jacqueline Fitzgerald, Carrie Hertan, Christine Font, Jenna Goldberg, Lauren Hall, Hillary Hirsch, Mona Li, Amy Mangus, Robert Marasco, Kimberly Marshall, Amy Migliaccio, Nina Mistry, Dave Rozzelle, Adriana Tierno, Alex Voznesenskiy, Vanessa Wu

· ·

ISBN 10: 1-60320-202-1, ISBN 13: 978-1-60320-202-2, ISSN: 1522-5895

Credits ■

FRONT COVER
(clockwise from top right) Getty Images; Chris Jackson/Getty Images; Lionel Hahn/Abaca USA; Michael Simon, Albert Ferreira/Startraks and Nick Saglimbeni; Bruce Glikas/Filmmagic; Pete Mariner/Retna/iPhoto

CONTENTS
2 (from top) Photoshot/EPA; Daniel Ochoa de Olza/AP; 3 (clockwise from top right) Brian Bowen Smith/August; Tony Duran/FOX; News Pictures/Wenn; DANNY MOLOSHOK/Reuters; Kevin Mazur/WireImage; Photofest

NEWS
4-5 Dimitar Dilkoff/AP; 6 Paul Gilham/Getty Images; 7 (clockwise from top) Christopher Furlong/Getty Images; Dominic Lipinski/AP; Chris Jackson/Getty Images; 8 (clockwise from top left) Andrew Winning/PA/AP; Gareth Fuller/PA/AP; Smart Pictures/Pacific Coast News; 9 (from top) Photoshot/EPA; Daniel Ochoa de Olza/AP; 10 Wally Santana/AP; 11 Kyodo/Xinhua/Zuma; 12 (clockwise from top) Orange County Sheriff's Office/AP; Brian Blanco/Landov; Red Huber/Orlando Sentinel/MCT/Landov; 13 (clockwise from top) Red Huber/AP; Phelan M. Ebenhack/AP(2); 14 (from top) Photofest; Everett; 15 Everett; 16 George Burns/Harpo/AP; 17 Eric Charbonneau/Wireimage; 18 Jim Smeal/BEImages; (inset) Imago/Zuma; 19 (from top) Max Nash/AFP/Getty Images; Facundo Arrizabalaga/EPA/Landov; Reuters; 20-21 Pete Souza/The White House/AP; (inset) AP; 22-23 Michael Doven/Getty Images; 24 Mark Shaw/MPTV Images; 26 Matt Sayles/AP; 27 Kevin Mazur/Wireimage; (insets from top) Ustream via Charlie Sheen/Pacific Coast News; Ryan Turgeon/Splash News; 28 Michael O'Neill/Corbis Outline; 29 (clockwise from top) Ted Aljibe/AFP/Getty Images; AP; Courtesy Andrew Jones; Courtesy Brown family; Courtesy Chris Campbell family; Courtesy Karen Kelly; Courtesy Bill Family; 30-31 (clockwise from right) Fabrizio Bensch/Reuters; Scanpix Norway/Reuters; Reuters(2); 32 (from top) Alison Dyer; Charles Dharapak/AP; NY Post/Splash News; 33 Erin Patrice O'Brien for the Wall Street Journal; 34 (from top) Kevin Mazur/Wireimage; Jason Willis; 35 Brian/National Photo Group; 36 (from top) Freddie Baez/Startraks; Carlo Allegri/AP; 37 Mary McCartney/Camera Press/Retna

TRAX

38-39 (clockwise from bottom left) Kevin Mazur/WireImage; Ethan Miller/Getty Images(2); 40 Mario Anzuoni/Reuters; 41 (clockwise from top left) MOE/Fame; Danny Moloshok/Reuters; TMZ/Splash News; 43 (clockwise from top left) Eric Charbonneau/Wireimage; 310pix; Ethan Miller/Getty Images; 44-45 (clockwise from top) Brian Doben; INF; James Veysey/Camera Press/Retna; Gretchen Le Maistre/Chronicle Books

CRIME
46-47 (clockwise from top right) Mirrorpix/Splash News; News Pictures/Wenn; Italian Polica/AP; Polaris; 48 (from top) NPR News Station/WBUR/Reuters; Boston Police via Boston Globe/AP; 49 Charlie Archambault/EPA/Landov; (insets from top) Justin Lane/EPA; Louis Lanzano/AP; 50 (clockwise from top left) Tasos Katopodis/Getty Images; Jim Urquhart/AP; Salt Lake County Sheriff/AP; Shawn Thew/EPA; 51 (from top) Danny Johnston/AP; Polaris

WEDDINGS
52-53 Robert Evans; 54-55 Eric Charbonneau; 56-57 Joe Buissink; 58 Robert Evans/Getty Images; 59 Ramey; 60 Xposure; 61 Jami Saunders; 62 Yvette Roman/Getty Images(3); 64 Joe Buissink; 65 Yitzhak Dalal/Hilton Media Group

SPLITS
66 Dave M. Benett/Wireimage; 67 (from top) Foto Manuele/Olycom/iPhoto; Evan Agostini/AP; 68 Kevin Winter/NBCU/Getty Images; Pena-Hall/INF; 69 Michael Simon, Albert Ferreira/Startraks and Nick Saglimbeni; 70 (from top) Matt Klitscher/ABC/Getty Images; Andrew Southam; 71 Christopher Polk/Getty Images; 72 Kevin Mazur/Wireimage; 73 Jerod Harris/Wireimage

BABIES
74-75 Photographs by Baby As Art; 76-77 Jeff Vespa/Getty Images; 78-79 Brian Bowen Smith/August; 80 Mike Disciullo/Bauer-Griffin; 81 Kurt Markus; 82 Donna Svennevik/Getty Images; 83 Maurizio La Pira/Splash News; 84 Brian Ach/AP; 85 Antoine Verglas; 86 (from top) Sasha/X 17; Splash News; 87 Andy Athineos/INF

MOVIES
88 Warner Bros.; 89 Everett; 90 (from top) Melinda Sue Gordon/Warner Bros.; Universal; Warner Bros.; 91 (from top) Everett; Roger Arpajou/Sony Pictures Classics

TV
92 Tony Duran/FOX; 93 Nino Munoz/FOX; 94 (from top) Splash News; Carol Kaelson/SONY; 95 (clockwise from top right) Ellen DeGeneres via

Twitter/Pacific Coast News; Andrew Southam/Icon Int'l; ABC Photo Archives/Getty Images; Ron Tom/ABC/Getty Images

MUSIC
96-97 Kristian Dowling/PictureGroup; 98 Lauren Dukoff/Columbia Records; 99 (from top) Mandi Wright/Detriot Free Press/MCT/Landov; Daniel Boczarski/Getty Images; 100 Steve Marcus/Reuters; 101 (clockwise from top right) GF/Bauer Griffin; Josiah Kamau/BuzzFoto; Jamie McCarthy/Wireimage; Kevin Mazur/Wireimage; John Shearer/Wireimage

FASHION
102-103 (from left)
Giulio Marcocchi/Sipa; Jeff Vespa/Wireimage; GF/Bauer Griffin; Peter West/Ace Pictures; 104-105 (from left) Lucas Jackson/Reuters; Danny Moloshok/Reuters; Lionel Hahn/Abaca USA; Jon Kopaloff/Filmmagic; Patrick Rideaux/PicturePerfect/Rex USA; Jason Merritt/Getty Images; 106-107 (clockwise from right) Fame; Albert Michael/Startraks; Splash News; KCSPresse/Splash News; Andy Kropa/Getty Images; 107 (coifs, from top) Marina Bay Sands/Getty Images; FOX; Robin Wong/PR Photos; Everett; Kevin Winter/Getty Images; Everett; 108-109 (clockwise from top right) Jim De Yonker/THE CW; Nathalie Lagneau/Catwalking/Getty Images; Vanderlei Almeida/AFP/Getty Images; Kevin Winter/Getty Images; Gary Hershorn/Reuters; Pascal Le Segretain/Getty Images; Gary Hershorn/Reuters; Michael Yada/©A.M.P.A.S.®.; Gary Hershorn/Reuters

TRIBUTES
110-111 Mattia Zoppellaro/Contrasto/Redux; 112 Lori Grinker/Contact Press Images; 113 Calo-MF/Abaca USA; 114 CBS Photo Archive/Getty Images; 115 CBS/Landov; 116 J. Vespa/Wireimage; 117 Bettmann/Corbis; 118 (from top) Globe; Peter Brooker/Rex USA; 119 Roger Ressmeyer/Corbis; 120 Neal Preston/Corbis; 121 Bob D'Amico/ABC/Getty Images; 122 Sunset Boulevard/Corbis; 124 (from top) Mychal Watts/Wireimage; Markus Schreiber/AP; 125 Jim Britt/ABC Photo Archives/Getty Images; 126 Brian Doben/Contour by Getty Images

BACK COVER
(clockwise from bottom left) Jamie McCarthy/Wireimage; Matt Sayles/AP; Universal; Robert Evans; Steffen Schmidt/EPA; James Veysey/Camera Press/Retna; Reuters; Jaap Buitendijk/Warner Bros.